# IRONDEQUOIT UNITED CHURCH OF CHRIST

# REFLECTIONS OF 100 YEARS

## By Juanita Tischendorf

# Contents

    This book is dedicated to the Ruth Circle who willingly supported this effort as well as becoming participants in the formation of the 2011 program to honor the Irondequoit United Church of Christ and its history.

    I also would like to dedicate this book to every minister past and present who has kept our church strong and healthy.  And, I dedicate this book to the congregation that inspired me to write the history of our church.

***Reflections of 100 Years***
***J. Tischendorf 2010***

It has been just over three years since I began my journey into the archives of our church, marveling at the history that surrounded me in that storage room and wondering if I could produce a book covering so much of the past and present. Until turning the key in the lock and entering the room, I had my doubts, but they soon dissipated as my heart and head filled with how incredibly preserved the details were. Each cabinet, each file drawer built the story for me and the more I unveiled, the more I wanted to know. By the end of the first year of research I was hooked.

I had no idea of the church being so embedded into the actual development of the town of Irondequoit and even history beyond our community. For instance a section of this building began as the Women's Christian Temperance Union (WCTU) and the building was their gift to our church. Even the streets and roads of Irondequoit bear the name of prominent individuals in the area who became members of the church that formed 'across the Ridge'. What drove these pioneers was Faith. Faith is a wonderful and powerful motivator.

After the first year it was so very easy to make trip after trip to sit, read and record information that I felt too fragile to remove from the premises. I took pleasure in touching documents that had been held by generations before me, enlightening me on what was a simpler time in our history. Each time I found a photograph of a minister or a member of the congregation I felt like a part of a family and the more I learned, it comforted me.

Just as I know there is always a beginning, even though it may not be as clearly defined as our church history was, I also know that this wonderful exploration would eventually end and it sorrowed me. I had become possessed with the fixation of being with these people of the past and didn't want to modernize the experience by putting it all into the computer. What a journey I was given!

Later as I keyed each page of information and viewed each picture, I knew that I had been drawn to this church for a reason I had not known before. First it is important to say that on the day that I and my husband first entered the  doors of IUCC it was frigid outside and inside too since the furnace wasn't working. In the sanctuary sat the congregation still dressed in their winter coats, gloves and hats as if this was natural. Yet, I sat down and found myself engulfed in the sermon, and later the people that made up the congregation. I was a member before I officially joined or officially learned that the church did have heat.

Each day as I began to shape the history of IUCC, I had a new appreciation of the streets, roads and avenues that snaked through our neighborhoods. I felt as though I knew Mr. Titus whose name appears on the avenue in front of the church. Even homes that I passed, like the Rudman Estate was much more than just an old house to me. I had become one with the history and now I wanted what I had learn to touch the hearts of others and if I could, allow this story to come into every home.

This inspirational story is of hope and opportunity that details what dedication and love of God can do for us. It is because of forceful individuals who gave of their time and talent that we can enjoy this church today and if we see them as our role models we can leave the same legacy for the future.

Sitting majestically on Titus Avenue in the suburb of West Irondequoit is a landmark that has housed so much of the history of the town and perhaps even the country as it grew over decades to become the Irondequoit United Church of Christ (IUCC). This church, in the year 2011, will celebrate its one hundred-year anniversary, though religious gatherings in a building that dates back to before the church began in 1911.

Actually, the United Church of Christ was formed in 1957 by a merger of the General Council of Congregational Christian Churches and the Evangelical and Reformed Church, so this century landmark is a melding of the past and the future—a union of one Christian organization offering their building and then relinquishing the property to the Congregational Church, which would later become what is now the United Church of Christ.

The church began from the first structure, built by and for the WCTU (Women's Christian Temperance Union), who would later graciously give their building as a gift to . What a wonderful gesture and how grateful we are to have this wonderful building today.

We are often reminded of our connection to the WCTU who began the Sabbath School Classes in this building in 1884. The section of the building where the Sabbath school classes met, still stands; thanks to brick and mortar, but that is another story. Yes, we have a rich history that has made us proud to present this 100 year centennial celebration edition of "Reflections"

# Women's Christian Temperance Union

Frances E. Willard
Second National President
(1879-1898)

In the small, picturesque village of Fredonia, New York, in Chautauqua County, a group of women came to hold their first meeting of the Women's Christian Temperance Union (WCTU) in 1873. This event happened at a time when suffragists were still alienating most American women, who viewed them as too radical a group to join or support even if their purpose was to gain rights for women. It would be women like Frances Elizabeth Caroline Willard (1839-1898) a prominent American temperance crusader and women's suffrage leader, born in Churchville, N.Y. who would play an important role in the growth of the WCTU.

Members of the group famous in our area were also well known around the country. There was Susan Brownell Anthony an outstanding women's rights leader with sharp political instincts, who met Elizabeth Cady Stanton, and together they took suffrage petitions door-to-door.  Later they would  recruit Carrie Catt and Anna Shaw to suffrage.  Living with her sister Mary in Rochester, NY, Susan B. Anthony became internationally respected as a symbol of the woman's movement.

Ms Willard later would become not only the most famous president of the WCTU, but the most famous 19th-century woman in America and perhaps even the world. Under Ms. Willard's leadership the WCTU was organized by women who were concerned about the destructive power of alcohol and the problems it was causing their families and society. They met in churches to pray and then marched to saloons to ask the owners to close their establishments.

**The Crusaders Brought Their Message To The Saloons**

The women would walk two by two singing, "Give to the Winds Thy Fears," a song that later became known to every WCTU member as the Crusade Hymn. Every day they visited saloons and drug stores where liquor was sold. They prayed on sawdust floors if they were allowed to enter. If not, they knelt on snowy pavements before the doorways until almost all the sellers surrendered. By the 1880s the WCTU was the largest organization of women in the United States.  It was described as "unquestionably the first mass movement of American women.  The WCTU succeeded in mobilizing large numbers of women and its members chose total abstinence from all alcohol as their lifestyle and adopted the definition of temperance as: ***"Moderation in all things healthful; total abstinence from all things harmful."***

The Symbol Of The WCTU

However, they were about more than abstinence. Among the WCTU's primary objectives in temperance reform was "protection of the home." Through education and example, the WCTU encouraged others to pledge total abstinence from alcohol and, later, tobacco and other drugs. They adopted a white ribbon bow to symbolize purity and a slogan to encompass their beliefs: *"Agitate - Educate - Legislate."*

This represents the beginning of the history of the building on Titus Avenue in Irondequoit, New York.

The next phase in the history began with the Congregational church. The Congregational church was designed so that each congregation would have a free hand in the control of its own affairs, the underlying principle for the church being that each local congregation has as its head Jesus alone and that the relations of the various congregations are those of fellow members in one common family of God.

Although by the end of the nineteenth century two-thirds of all Congregationalists still resided in New England, the denomination's early leadership in foreign missions, abolitionism, and women's rights testified to its powerful and generally progressive role as cultural arbiters. In the late nineteenth century, Congregationalists like Washington Gladden1[1] and Josiah Strong[2] led the Social Gospel movement's call for social action among Protestant churches.

Sometime after the Congregational church, the present denomination came into existence. Although the United Church of Christ (UCC) is a relatively young Protestant denomination, formed in 1957, the historical roots of its four constituent bodies have been around for a long time. The UCC brought together the Congregational Christian Church—itself the product of a 1931 union of Congregationalist and Christian churches that originated in 1794—with the Evangelical and Reformed church—the product of a 1934 merger

---

[1] A leading American Congregational church pastor and early leader of the Social Gospel Movement.
[2] Protestant clergyman and author who was a founder of the Social Gospel movement.

between the German Reformed and Evangelical Synod churches that originated in 1817. This diverse historical background encompasses Calvinism, American revivalism and German pietism, but to a considerable degree the four traditions have shared a common commitment to social witness and ecumenical efforts toward Christian unity. The Bible was to be their only arbiter of practice and teaching, and the unity of all believers their final goal.  The constitution for the new body was adopted in July 1961, thus completing the union.

This is how the church body came into being, but there is more to the story on how it reached the suburb of Irondequoit.

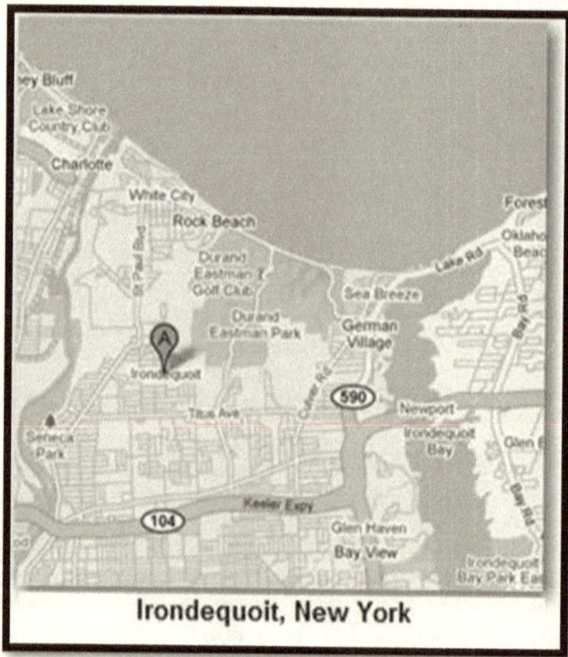


**Irondequoit, New York**

The town of Irondequoit lies between the Genesee River on the west and Irondequoit Bay on the east, with the northern border of the town being defined by the shoreline of Lake Ontario. Aware of its unique geography, one can understand why this name was chosen, since Irondequoit aptly means "where the land and waters meet."During the last part of the 19th century, the northern edge of the town was developed as a tourist and vacation area for the City of Rochester residents and was once known as the "Coney Island of Western New York."

Originally, Irondequoit was part of the suburb of Brighton. When Irondequoit was separated from Brighton in 1839, the newly-elected school commissioners divided the town into four school districts. District Number 1 occupied the southwest part of the township, later to be known as the Bell School District; District Number 2, the northeast part; District Number 3, the northwest part; District Number 7, the southeast section, which was given that number because it was a part of Brighton District Number 7 and would be known as the Brighton-Irondequoit District for some years.

## Stephen Titus Plays A Role

Stephen B. Titus was born on the homestead in the town of Irondequoit, in 1849. He was educated in the public schools and had been a market gardener all his life. His father, George W. Titus, was born in Canada in 1820, and the family came to the United States in 1823, locating near Scottsville where he was educated in the public schools, and in 1834 they moved to the town of Irondequoit. He married Sophia Oyler, of London, England, by whom he had six children. Stephen had somewhere around twenty-two acres of garden in a high state of cultivation, and served in partnership with his brother, Frank C., under the firm name of S. S. Titus & Bro

The earliest schoolhouse, built in District Number 3, was of logs. It stood on the southeast corner of Titus Avenue and Lower Hudson (now Cooper Road) on land donated by Stephen Titus in 1840. This log school was used until 1861, when a one-room brick school built on the opposite corner of Titus and Lower Hudson Avenues replaced it.

Sabbath School met in the two-room District 3 school (right foreground) from 1861 until the W.C.T.U. Hall (left background) was built in 1884.

## The Grants Do their Part

But it was the Grant's kitchen that became one of the first classrooms for children and adults who wanted to learn how to read and write. During the day one could witness children studiously at work on their lessons, while at night at that same table sat parents wanting to learn the 3R's so that they would not prove to be an embarrassment to their children.

The picture below was taken in 1876; the Grants, Sidney and Adeline, are in the center (Sidney standing and Adeline seated next to him). Their oldest son, Frank, is on the left, with his wife, Eva Dake Grant, next to him. Eva was also from an old pioneer family. Her father, Charles Dake, was one of Irondequoit's first doctors.

**Sidney & Adeline Grant appear in the center of this old photo.**

Finally on the right is Mate Wilson, a boarder who was a tailoress in one of the early clothing factories, and the child on the rocking horse was Frank and Eva's son, Pierce.

What was to happen in the town of Irondequoit came about as a result of the dedication of three women. On a lovely springtime day, two ladies drove along Little Ridge (Titus Avenue) to call on a friend on Garden Street (Portland Avenue), and together the three decided that what the growing young town needed most of all was a Sabbath School. Although the families of those early days were members of Rochester churches, there was no Sunday school north of Ridge Road so far as local religious services were concerned, and it was this need that Mrs. C. Woodworth, Mrs. H. S. Hagaman and Mrs. S. B Grant were determined to change.

## The Sabbath School Is Born

This group of women set about gathering small groups of children to join the Sabbath School, which at first met in several of the farm homes with their leaders, with others at various other homes, and even in large barns. Sabbath school was a discipleship through religious education and so much more  In seeking to meet the spiritual needs of its members, Sabbath School featured emphasis on fellowship, outreach, Bible study, and mission.  It hope to provide a rich spiritual environment in practical everyday settings.

The Sabbath school became a hit!  In a very short time the attendance grew so large that it was necessary to meet in the old one-room, red schoolhouse on the northeast corner of Cooper Road and Little Ridge.

Located across the road stood the newly completed Grange Hall that would also become temporary quarters for the Sabbath School.  Granges, also known as "The Order of the Patrons of Husbandry back in the day, had been envisioned as a secret society, with passwords, secret signals and other covert means of identification.  Membership was supposed to be open to farmers and their families, although at one point, lawyers, businessmen and politicians joined the ranks seeking favoritism. This expanded granges into the  urban areas as well as rural areas.

***

The Sabbath School was not a place only for children.  Townspeople of all ages and denominations were called to worship, as the effort was to bring people together in the rural community.  While Mrs. Woodworth, Mrs. Hagaman and Mrs. Grant volleyed for the soul, from the first town meeting in Irondequoit in 1839 the establishment of schools became of primary importance.  Frontiersmen who had not had the advantage of schooling were determined to give that advantage to their children, while they harbored the hope that it would provide them an opportunity to learn as well.

Mrs. Sidney B. Grant

Adeline Grant, along with her husband, Sidney, quickly became an important part of the Irondequoit community and the Grants were charter members of the Sunday school classes. Sidney Grant also served as a trustee of school district #3, while Mrs. Grant was President of the Women's Christian Temperance Union (WCTU).

No bigger advocates of church and school were there than the Grant family. 1847, Sidney Grant gave up his role as a teacher and moved to Irondequoit, purchasing a farm at what is now 3219 St. Paul Boulevard. In His wife, Adeline, was also a teacher. Even though they had given up their professions, neither had gave up their interest in education.

Just as dedicated to the cause was Mrs. Hagaman, who wanted more for the community and was willing to work hard to achieve what she sensed was needed. At the start she felt that to properly organize a Sabbath school, one must have a library. When she voiced her opinion, she found she was not alone in her thinking, so along with Mrs. Woodworth and Mrs. Silas Briggs, they made calls at every home in the area to invite the children of each family to come to Sabbath School and to ask for contributions for a library. The day they set about collecting for the library was horse-racing day in Irondequoit, so they encountered only one man at home. That did not stop them; what they found was that the women who were home gave generously.

And so it was that on Sunday, May 5, 1850, Mr. Samuel W. Lee, an elder of Brick Presbyterian Church and one of the more active Sabbath school organizers in Monroe County, came down from the city to establish the Irondequoit Sabbath School and agreed to act as the superintendent. One more joy came their way when Mr. Lee's son, the librarian at Brick Church, offered his assistance in the selection of books purchased with the library fund, which amounted to $15.00, a generous sum in those days.

The word was getting out, and the town showed their support on the Sunday after the collection; thirty-two children and nine teachers were present, and just a week later fifty-one people attended the new Sabbath School. The Sabbath School was growing fast.

The original minutes book that contained the records of the Sabbath School from its start in 1850 until 1856 noted that Mr. Sidney B. Grant was elected superintendent in May of 1851 and that Mr. and Mrs. Woodworth, along with Mrs. Hagaman, were among the ten teachers. Along with this responsibility, Mr. Woodworth also served as assistant superintendent.

Other details recorded were simply informal, as these were simple times. One can read in the record books, for instance, that on Sunday, October 19, 1851, "Not any school today, it was very rainy." Then on September 11, 1853, it was noted , "No preaching today, no superintendent."

## First Attempt For A Union Church

In 1854 an attempt was made to form a Union church in the town of Irondequoit, north of the Ridge, but though the farmers found journeying all the way into town a struggle, out of loyalty they continued to attend services there but willingly attended Sabbath school in the afternoons in Irondequoit. The names in the records at the start of the Sabbath school were Benedict, Blossom, Forest, Grant, Hagaman, Rogers, Sherry and Woodworth. These names continued in the records as their descendants became charter members of the church.

This was the first proposal for a Union church, but loyalty to city churches prevailed and no action was taken. Only this did not deter the Sabbath School founders, who took it on as a challenge.

During the first six years, the school saw major growth in attendance. Where there had been twelve members, there were seventy-five. The top collection made on a single Sunday was seventy-five cents, and the lowest was eight cents.

In the beginning, the Sabbath School services were held in the afternoon and only during the summer months. The school closed in October and was reconvened in May of the following year. In the evenings there was preaching by visiting clergymen from Rochester churches and by students from the young Rochester Theological Seminary, the forerunner of the Colgate-Rochester Divinity School. Determination was winning out as attendance continued its upward swing, eventually requiring a change in the Sabbath School schedule. A year-round program was desired.

The Founders Of The Irondequoit Chapter of the Women's Christian Temperance Union (WCTU)

## Birth Of The Irondequoit Chapter Of WCTU

Not afraid to step up and take the next step, these women realized that there was a need for more involvement and so in 1880 they decided to organize the Irondequoit Chapter of the Women's' Christian Temperance Union. The WCTU was organized at a meeting at School Number 3 on the corner of Cooper Road and Titus Avenue. The founding members were Mrs. S. B. Grant, grandmother of Frank

Grant, Mrs. Gideon Anthony, a cousin of Susan B. Anthony, Mrs. H. Atwater, Mrs. C. H. Stanton, Mrs. German Titus, Mrs. Alonzo Payne and Mrs. Isaac Waring. These ladies formed the nucleus of a group of forty-two charter members with Mrs. Grant elected president. Although Susan B. Anthony was supportive of the Rochester women organizers of the WCTU, she told them that women would need to get the vote to reach their goal, so she did not officially join the group.

***

Widespread religious fervor was a central feature of the Temperance and Prohibition eras. In the early nineteenth century, a religious revival known as the Second Great Awakening took the nation by storm, with preachers announcing that the millennium lay at hand, men and women began to swear off hard spirits.

From 1880 until 1884, the Sabbath School continued to be held in the two-room District 3 School, but then a miracle happened. The Curtice family gave land to the WCTU to erect a building. That gift, along with funds solicited from the entire town, went toward erecting a building that would be dedicated to temperance and religious work. The original WCTU Hall was built at a cost of $5,000.00 and accommodated the growing Sabbath school. This building occupied a part of the site of the present-day United Church of Christ building. The Sabbath School moved into its new building in 1885.

Temperance Sundays were held once each quarter, and they helped the WCTU present its message and strengthened the bond between it and the Sabbath School. No doubt this tie greatly strengthened both groups and certainly provided the Sabbath school with a building and opportunities that would not have been possible without the joint support.

WCTU Hall, Irondequoit NY (1884 - 1909)

When the WCTU was officially occupying the new building, the need for a piano was met by Mr. Frederick Starr, and the first piano he ever made was placed in the building and a custom was born around this time.

Frederick Starr was a resident of Rochester who lived here before or during the civil war. Mr. Starr was born in Warren, Connecticut and his schoolmates included his cousin, Charles G. Finney, the famous evangelist, and Horace Bushnell, the noted preacher. At the age of twenty he went was a clerk in a bookstore in New York and two years later came to Rochester where he began the manufacture of furniture, being the pioneer in what has become one of our major industries, and building up a large business, which he would give up in 1850 to enter upon the manufacture of pianos.

Each student enrolled in the Sabbath School had to pay for a chair and a hymn book.  At the end of each day, the students were required to take their chair home with them and bring them back the next time. No one, it is known, voiced a complaint nor in any way did this custom of purchasing a chair and a hymn book slow the growth of the Sabbath School.

Once every quarter a Temperance Sunday was held by the WCTU and on Wednesday nights there was prayer meetings for the

Sabbath School.  The cooperative project between the Sabbath School and the WCTU was working.

A large group along with the responsibility of the upkeep of the building was dependent on the collections taken to keep afloat.  The collections were now averaging around five dollars each Sunday, and with much of the equipment for the new building being provided as gifts from the classes, the expenses were kept under control. Since this was a joint venture, many of the incoming funds were designated specifically for the WCTU organization or for the Sabbath School.

Growth is what was sought after, and growth continued until the Sabbath school was again outgrowing the space available in their new building. By 1887, there were more than two hundred students attending Sabbath school, so the WCTU decided it was time to enlarge the Hall.  Now came the issue of where to hold the Sabbath School while the building was under construction.

## George Rudman Steps Up To The Plate

David Rudman, father of George., was born in Malmsbury, England married Eliza Porter of his native place, and had ten children, four of whom were born in England: The family came to the United States in 1848, and located in the town of Irondequoit. George's brother William was born in the town of Irondequoit,. He was educated in the public schools, after which he engaged in market gardening. He became town assessor for three years, and in 1877, he married Hattie L. Stanton of Irondequoit.  They would have four children.

George was just as interested in being a part of his community as his family had been before him.  His support was soon to be recognized when he stepped up as yet another guardian angel, offering the carriage house on their farm, located on Portland Avenue, as a meeting place for the WCTU and the Sabbath school.  There was a custom established in the early days of the Sabbath school, and that was to name the classes after the person in charge.  George Rudman served as the Superintendent of the Sabbath School, but also had a class named after him.

When construction was completed on the WCTU building, the Sabbath School and the WCTU occupied the building once again, and the arrangement between the two organizations remained intact for more than two decades.

# The Late 1800s

The late 1800s were an era of progress in America.  Westward
expansion was completed, new states were joining the country, and
manufacturing, communication, and transportation were bringing the
United States to world power status. Churches also were showing
progress. There were more new members than ever in all
denominations, not just total numbers but in proportion to the increase
in population. Interdenominational cooperation was beginning to
happen, and foreign mission projects were reaching a high point of
success

Congregationalists were beginning to feel the need for national
unity, so in 1870 the national Pilgrim Memorial Convention was held
in Chicago to celebrate the 250th anniversary of the landing of the
Pilgrims at Plymouth.  One of the resolutions that the convention
produced was for individual state Congregational associations to work
toward the formation of a permanent national body.  The result was that
in November of 1871, a meeting was held in Oberlin, Ohio, at which
the National Council of Congregational Churches was formed.

The members of the National Council were very careful to
keep within the polity of historical Congregationalism.  Membership
was divided between clergy and laymen on an almost equal basis.  The
Council acted as a "*Council Of Reference*" so as not to violate local
Congregational autonomy.

It was a time in our country's history when the cities were
swelling with immigrants from all corners of the world, and many
Congregational churches followed their members as they moved away
from the city.  In 1874 another attempt was made to form a Union
Church in Irondequoit, but again the attempt failed.

The Rochester pastors of several denominations continued to
visit the Sabbath School frequently, preaching at afternoon services. A
series of revival meetings were held in 1857 and another was held in
1877 that intensified religious fervor and developed an increased desire
for "*Stated Worship And Regular Preaching*" in the Irondequoit
community.

***

Standing on the steps of the W.C.T.U. Starting from the left: Walter Mulcock, William Killick, Henry Franke, James H. West, III, John W. Peacock, Norton Barnes, Louise Rayton, Lyda Laming, George N. Peacock, Martha Stutton, Richard Metcalf, Lottie Laming, Martha Hill, Edward Hallauer and Charles Dunbar

In 1895 the original one-room schoolhouse was demolished and a more modern four-room building took its place. In 1898 the Irondequoit District No. 3 School became Irondequoit Union Free School, but more changes were in the wind. This is what eventually led to afternoon Sabbath School sessions.

## Sabbath School & WCTU GROW

Like the Sabbath School, the WCTU experienced growth, which led to their erecting a building to house its activities, starting with fundraising. Each effort to reach out gave back threefold to the Sabbath School. The library started by the founders of the Sabbath School back in 1850 continued in importance and had a noticeable influence on attendance, since for many years only those who enrolled in the Sabbath School could borrow books. When there was talk of expanding the library, the classes sponsored a musical and literary entertainment event in 1898 to raise funds to put the library on a more useful basis.

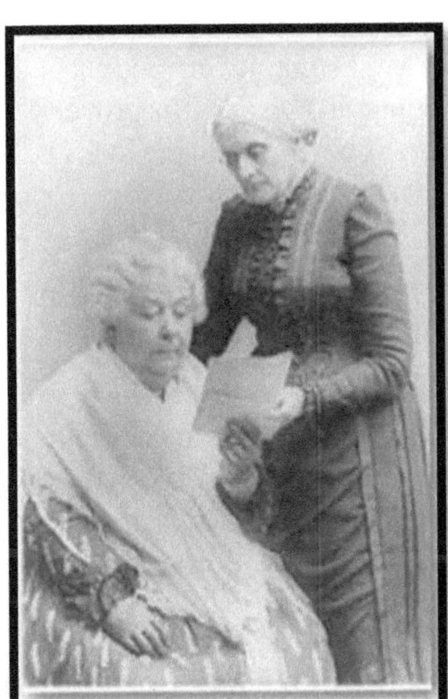

Susan B. Anthony (Standing) & Elizabeth Cady Stanton (Seated)

The Sabbath School and the WCTU engaged in many money-raising events to support their separate and combined interests, such as socials, luncheons and a Temperance Tea Party. It was often hard to determine which Christian endeavor had been initiated by which group, but even with their many common aims and many interlocking memberships, the two were still distinct and independent organizations.

Susan B. Anthony was born in South Adams, Massachusetts in 1820. Her father, Daniel Anthony, a cotton manufacturer, educated his daughter by private teachers to be self-supporting.

Her education was completed at a Friends' boarding school in Philadelphia and in 1845 her father settled in Rochester where two years later his daughter made her first public speech, the subject being temperance. From that time she worked in the cause of temperance and other public reforms. In 1851 she called a temperance convention in Albany, having been refused admission to a previous convention because of her sex. In 1852, assisted by Elizabeth Cady Stanton, they organized the Woman's New York State Temperance society. Here chief work became women equal political rights to those enjoyed by men, In 1868, associated with Elizabeth Cady Stanton, Parker Pillsbury and George Francis Train, she began the publication in New York city of a weekly paper called The Revolution, and devoted to the enfranchisement of women. and e published the History of Woman Suffrage, in three volumes. When, in 1891, Mrs. Stanton retired from the presidency of the National American Woman Suffrage association, Miss Anthony was chosen as her successor.

It was when Susan B. Anthony worked to start a Political Equality Group that she chanced to meet Mrs. Hunt; it was said that Miss Anthony had asked who the prim young lady was. This proved that although the differences between the suffragettes and the WCTU were still quite visible, there was respect and acceptance shown.

The influence of the Sabbath School could be seen everywhere. An early desire to bring religion into the homes of permanent shut-ins gave birth to the establishment in 1902 of the House Department under the direction of Miss Mary Moall.

The group included the distribution of materials such as lesson quarterlies and magazines delivered by a large corps of volunteers. John Callister, who served as the Sunday School chorister[3] from 1870-1901, retired and was given a gold cane to commemorate his years of dedicated service. Over the years John had given more than just his talents. He had given the stone for the building in 1884 and after retiring from this position was elected Chorister Emeritus, receiving the same pay he had always had.

Giving was what it was all about. Many people supported the Sabbath School, and no less support came from within the Sabbath School itself. The Rudman class, in 1901 presented a bookcase to the school that had cost $54.00. Other classes also offered their gifts, and the Sabbath School needs were constantly being met.

***

Smallpox was a frequent visitor to the cities of the world. Minor outbreaks threatened the city in 1833, 1845, 1863, 1873, and 1895, but did not become full scale epidemics. Smallpox was unique amongst dreaded infectious diseases and it could be prevented by either inoculation or vaccination. Inoculation, dating from the 18th century, consisted of introducing an infected smallpox scab under the skin. The recipient, if fortunate, developed a mild case of smallpox and would thereafter be immune to the disease. If unfortunate, the recipient soon fell ill with smallpox in full force. This could mean disfigurement and even death, and there was no way to know which to expect. Inoculation therefore entailed serious risk. Vaccination replaced inoculation around 1800, following its discovery by Edward Jenner, an English doctor.

---

[3] A leader of a choir

In 1902, the city experienced a major outbreak of smallpox. This epidemic brought the city to the edge of disaster and only a program of community-wide vaccination halted the spread of this dreaded infectious disease. Thanks to the efforts, of health and local officials this would be the last smallpox epidemic in the city, but before the disease was under control, 100 had died.

In 1902 the records of the Sabbath School noted that the school was being closed from November 23 to 30 on account of a contagious disease,. During this period, Mrs. Edith Heffer's class spent the year doing Home Missions work and provided a dinner for a shut-in family.

The First Chapel in the Old W.C.T.U. Hall

In 1903 the work of the Sabbath School was carried on by classes that gave pennies as an offering for missionary work, and such events played an important role in the growth in size of the classes. At one point Mrs. Benjamin Franke's class was divided, and Miss Stella Stanton took charge of the new class that was formed. In 1904 the Sabbath school teachers included Mr. Lake, Mr. G. H. Rudman, Mr. Franke, Mr. John Howard, Mr. John Heffer, Mr. H. B. Killde, Mr. Morgan, Mr. James Howard, Mrs. B. Franke, Mrs. F. Metcalf, Miss Sherry, Miss Rayton, Miss Cateau, Mrs. A. Franke, Mrs. B. Coy, Mrs. S. H. Killick, Mrs. George Heffer, Mrs. Camping, Mrs. S. Heffer, Miss Thompson and Miss Harding.  By 1905 the average attendance had reached 213.

# Two Room Addition Added In Early 1900

By 1907 the district purchased two more acres of land for the sum of $1,250 from Mr. Charles Howard to add on a two-room addition to the building one year later. In the interim, the Sunday classes met in the District 3 School building (Irondequoit Union School), which was built in 1895 on the site of the two-room schoolhouse that had been used as a meeting place for the Sabbath School.  The WCTU formed a committee to canvas the town for members, and their efforts were rewarded with eighty-seven new members joining the school, which was mostly made up of people who were related to each other.

Mr. David Cheney organized his class as the Dorcas Class and during the holiday season the class administered to those in need by providing Thanksgiving and Christmas dinners.  Mrs. Spencer Heffer's class gave $4.82 for missionary work and sent donations to shut ins, and made comforters for the needy, while Miss West's class organized a Thanksgiving dinner for a needy family in the town.  Each member pledged 5 cents per month for mite boxes which were also called alms box or poor box.  The mite boxes were used to save coins for charitable purposes.

# WCTU Building Destroyed By Fire

Then at 2:00 a.m. on October 29, 1909, the WCTU Hall was destroyed by fire, and with it all the records of the Sabbath School that were stored on the premises. The fire occurred the morning after the WCTU had held its Annual Harvest Supper and Apron Sale in the Hall, which had yielded a  profit of around eighty dollars.  The fire destroyed the inside of the brick building as well as all of the equipment.  It was thought that the fire may have started from some defective gas heat arrangement that had just been installed, but that could not be verified.

**This became only a temporary setback, as it did not affect the determination of these women as they set about planning the building of a new hall, at which time the idea of a church took form. These women of the Sabbath School and the WCTU were brave and determined souls. Within twelve hours following the fire, the officers of both organizations held meetings. The Sabbath School group met at Mrs. Reuben A. Dake's home, and the members of the WCTU met at the schoolhouse. The groups also met together to begin plans for a new structure. It was at these individual and group meetings that the need for a church in Irondequoit was discussed in earnest.**

## Hosea Rogers Gets Involved

In 1836, Captain Rogers purchased a farm of eighty-five acres in what is now the town of Irondequoit and in that year was married and settled on his farm. which remained his home from that time until his death. Later he sailed for two years, but returned home to take charge of his farm.

Soon after locating to Irondequoit he became interested in the building of sailing vessels, will still keeping his farm operational. The Captain was also actively identified with the business interests of Rochester, eventually becoming president of the PHELPS & ROGERS LUMBER COMPANY on Warehouse street.

Captain Rogers was married, in October, 1837, to Miss Polly VAN DUSEN, who died January 25, 1871, and on the 1st of May, 1873, he wedded Miss Mary J. LYON, of Albion, New York, who departed this life May 25, 1875. He was again married February 2,

1876, his third union being with Miss Asenath Scholfeld, of Port Colborne, Canada, whose grandparents came originally from England. Her grandfather, John Scholfeld, was a farmer by occupation and a veteran of the war of 1812. He died in 1866. Her father, James Scholfeld, was collector of Port Colborne, Ontario, for thirty-three consecutive years and died in 1889. Captain Scholfeld and his third wife would have five children: Polly M., at home; William H., of the Genesee lumberyard, who married Carrie D. Rollison and lives in Rochester; Luella A., Ezra S. And Alida J., all at home.

***

Mrs. Cooper and Mrs. Titus placed themselves in charge of collecting the money to pay for the new WCTU Hall and went to discuss the matter with Mrs. Hunt's father, Hosea Rogers[4]. They informed him of the need to raise the funds to rebuild their building and the current situation of the drive for funds. Mr. Rogers listened intently and when they were done, he said he would be supportive and told them to go ahead with their building plans as he would gladly back them.

***

In the 1910s, there was conservative religious revival in the United States that had a back to basics approach to religion. Prohibition provided political backing and legitimacy for the religious revival that promoted abstinence and the Christian fundamentalists held their ground regarding their anti-drinking crusade.

The morals and values that the religious revivals of the Temperance and Prohibition Eras promoted helped with the fund raising. With all the efforts to attract members paying off, the need for even larger quarters again was obvious and along with the support of Mr. Rogers, the Sabbath school and the WCTU put their heads together. They were determined to raise monies for the building project.

***

---

[4] Hosea Rogers was a pioneer and Lake Captain who settled in Irondequoit and built his home in 1852. Known as the "Great Lakes Sea Captain", Hosea Rogers was in the business of transporting grain from Chicago to Rochester.

The members of the Sabbath School gave a presentation of
"Ten Nights In a Bar Room" as one of the projects to raise money for
the new building. . As part of the strategy of the temperance movement,
theatrical plays were created to promote social reform.. These became
known as temperance plays. *Ten Nights in a Bar Room and What I Saw
There* was originally a novel by the popular nineteenth-century author
Timothy Shay Arthur. "Ten Nights in a Bar Room" became one of the
most popular temperance plays of the nineteenth century. The play
itself is very sentimental and melodramatic. One of the most prominent
songs in the work is the temperance ballad "Father, Dear Father, Come
Home with Me Now," known popularly as "The Song of the
Drunkard's Child," in which a child named Mary comes to an untimely
end because of her father's ways, sending out a moral message. Other
songs, such as "Farewell to Brandy, Rum, and Toddy," sung to the tune
of "Yankee Doodle Dandy," were also added to the play.

They also presented a more recent play, "The Golden Chain" (1907) by Y.L Peretz, which portrays three generations of a Hasidic[5] court that are on the verge of annihilation. The play opens with the last generation, Rabi Moishe, who is desperately trying to invoke his ancestors to come to his rescue and help him lead the congregation, but he is a weak leader and incapable of saving his court. As this happens in flashback scenes, the play goes back to the home of his grandfather, Rabi Shlomo, and his father, Rabi Pinchas. Because of the difficulty of this last play, help came from downtown Rochester to aid in the rehearsing for the presentation, and those who came to see the play deemed the results a success. This proved to be a great fundraiser, along with the added joy of meeting two prominent Rochester celebrities: Edwin Howard and Edna Anthony.

Through the persistent efforts of the women of the WCTU and the Sabbath School and the cooperation of the townspeople, the necessary funds were raised; the happy cooperation between the two

---

[5] Hasidic Judaism (also Chasidic, etc., from the Hebrew: חסידות , Chassidus, meaning "piety", from the Hebrew root word חסד chesed meaning "loving kindness") is a Haredi Jewish religious movement. Some refer to Hasidic Judaism as Hasidism, and the adjective chasidic / hasidic (or in Yiddish חסידיש khasidish) applies. The movement originated in Eastern Europe (what is now Belarus and Ukraine) in the 18th century.

groups continued with each helping to strengthen the other and together presenting a strong moral influence in the town.

As the work progressed on the new building, in the fall of 1910 the classes were moved into the basement of the unfinished structure.

## Dake & Rudman Spearhead The Project

Throughout the process, two men worked hard together to get the new hall erected: Reuben A. Dake and George H. Rudman. By this time Reuben A. Dake had already provided forty-three years of service to the Sabbath School.

He was a teacher and officer of the school and inspired and supported the plans to erect the new Hall. His dedication to not only the Sabbath School but also the Irondequoit community is apparent by the fact that the school on Cooper Road would bear his name.

Rueben A. Dake

Mr. Rudman owned quite an expanse of property in Irondequoit, where he farmed and raised his large family.  It was the men of this caliber who were the backbone of the growth of the Sabbath School by supporting the women's efforts. Without such strong support, the twenty-five- year mark might not have been reached with such success.

The cornerstone (or foundation stone) concept was derived from the first stone set in the construction of a masonry foundation. This was of importance since all other stones were set in reference to this stone, thus determining the position of the entire structure.  But over time a cornerstone became a ceremonial masonry stone, or replica, set in a prominent location on the outside of a building, with an inscription on the stone indicating the construction dates of the building and the names of architect, builder and other significant individuals. The rite of laying a cornerstone is an important cultural component of western architecture and metaphorically in sacred architecture generally.

This importance was placed on placing the W.C.T.U. Hall cornerstone on the building addition of 1910.

The Presentation of the W.C.T.U. Cornerstone

Looking back many Americans like to think of the first 18 years of our century as the "age of innocence." The time of gaslight horse and buggy lifestyle seemed to fit the name, but a closer look at the era would reveal the emergence of mass production, the Progressive movement, radical changes in the arts and of course a world war. This made the decade a time of rapid change and profound new experiences.

In 1911, the construction of the WCTU Hall was well underway. John Callister, who was the Sabbath School chorister, stepped forward to provide stone from his farm for the walls of the building. This stone was special in that it could not be found anywhere else in Irondequoit. Before the new WCTU Hall was completed, plans were underway to organize a church. During the early months of 1911, a meeting was held in the new WCTU Hall at which the Reverend Harold S. Capron, minister of the South Congregational Church in Rochester, advised the group of the steps they would need to perform to become a church family.

## Irondequoit Union Congregational Church

The United Congregational Church of Irondequoit (Irondequoit United Church of Christ) became a historic Congregational church complex that would consist of three interconnected buildings: the Colonial Revival style church (1926), Woman's Christian Temperance Union hall (1910), and church school

# Membership
*in the*
## Congregational Church

### As a Church Member

I believe in God the Father and in Jesus Christ, His
Son.
I believe in the work our Lord came to earth to do.
I believe in my church as the agency to carry on His
work.
I believe in myself as responsible for my share in the
service of my church.

### What is Christ's Work?

The teaching of the Fatherhood of God and the
Brotherhood of Man.
The expression of brotherhood in service,—healing the
sick; opening prison doors of ignorance; lifting the
burdens of sin and superstition.

### What is My Share in This Work?

I must know what my church is doing and how.
I must love my fellowmen of all races and lands as
Christ has loved me.
I must give as God has given me of time and strength
and money.
I must pray for the coming of the Kingdom of God and
believe in the power of our Lord working through me
to bring it to pass.

*These principles are enlarged in the following pages*

One hundred people were present, and Mr. Dake acted as chairman. The Covenant of the Congregational Church was adopted and committees were appointed.

The official name selected was the Irondequoit Union Congregational Church, and sixty-two names were enrolled as prospective members. The Reverend Harold Capron of Rochester was called as pastor of the church, and a Board of Deacons was established that included Reuben A. Dake, William Hill, Frank Heffer, Joseph Rayton, James Howard and George H. Rudman..

A Board of Trustees was also established that included Abram Frank, Thomas Pengelly, John Heifer, Seymore Titus, James Pammenter, and Almond Warren By the time the new hall was completed, the church had more than nine hundred members. In 1911 the deed was given to the Sabbath School. Mr. Dake presided, Pastor B.P. Richardson read the scripture, and the Rev. A. Lotee offered the dedicatory prayer.

Adding onto the WCTU Building

On January 24, 1911 at the Preliminary meeting, a motion was made that the church be named the Union Congregational Church of Irondequoit. Then on February 9, 1911 at the organization meeting, the Rev. Capron read the Covenant of the Congregational Church and advised that the Sabbath School adopt the covenant as read. The motion carried to adopt, in an informal way, the covenant as a whole, noting changes.

On February 27, 1911 at the Meeting of Church Committee, it was stated that although several laws had already been adopted at a previous church meeting, it was thought best that the committee take up and discuss all laws that appear in the Council Manual for a Congregational church. The committee agreed to advise that the church adopt the laws as they appeared in the Council Manual, with the exception that *the voting age shall be 18 except at a meeting of trustees when the voting age shall be 21*. The committee, however, did not act upon Article 8, Section 1, Paragraph 2, deeming it advisable the church discuss this matter before acting upon same. This article read as follows: "When to observe the Lord's Supper." It was also thought advisable that the church discuss Article 8, section 2, paragraph 5 before adopting it. This article stated that "*At the annual and all special meetings, ___ members shall be necessary to constitute a quorum for the transaction of business.*" A motion was passed in March of 1911 making the first Wednesday in March the date for the annual meeting of the church.

**1910 - BUILDING COMMITTEE**
**CHAIRMAN : ALBERT J. BRISTOL**

This was an official church housed in the building that began as the WCTU. The United Congregational Church of Irondequoit was growing in size and becoming a major part of the town with the church and Sabbath school and all activities taking place in the WCTU Hall. A librarian and his assistant were added as officers of the Sabbath school, and their efforts went into finding hymn books, scripts and petition books.

Although the first name chosen for the new church was Union Congregational Church of Irondequoit, at a later meeting this was changed to United Congregational Church of Irondequoit.

An effort was made to interest the people of Central Chapel (in the Culver Road area) to join the new church, but this did not succeed, so the Central Chapel group later became Irondequoit Presbyterian Church. From the very start their interest was in participating in the Sabbath School, and each class, having its own name, would come up with fundraiser ideas. The Dorcas Class, which was form by the Alice Baker Class, Mrs. Colt's Class, and Jennie Rudman's Class, put on a mock wedding, which was quite a successful fundraiser. But with all the changes, the traditions of the Sabbath School and the individual classes continued.

## Tom Thumb Wedding

This would be one of the many efforts that were presented and successfully implemented by the Sabbath school members to raise money for the new building.  Presented as a mock wedding performed by the Dorcas Class, the performance was successful in raising funds. It also gave the class a way to participate in this venture.

**Dorcas Class, Mock Wedding**

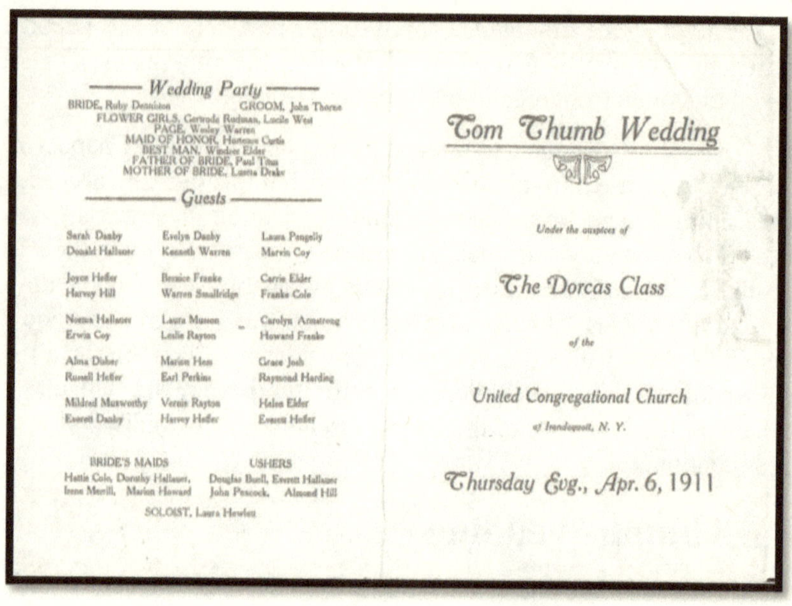


It being a simple time in our history many of the records were simplistic.  Take for instance the notations in the WCTU minutes after the plans of the new hall had been shown and discussed.

"It was decided that we accept the complete plans and that we let the advisory committee do whatever they think is best to put it into a contractors hands.

WCTU building fund disbursements:
June - to the architect - $100.00
June - to the mason - $270.00
July - to the contractor - $1250.00
July 14, 1910: Mrs. George West spoke of having a tablet to mark the hall.  It was moved to let the building committee take charge of the matter.
Sept. 6, 1910: Have had subscribed $5,598.00 toward paying for the new hall - Which is being erected.
Nov. 16, 1910: First use made of the new hall by the Sabbath School - in the basement.
Dec.10, 1910: The hall is used for a Christmas program.
Jan. 22, 1911 Hall dedicated."

# Rev. Harold Capron (1911-1916)

Around May of 1911, the United Congregational Church issued a call to the Reverend Harold S. Capron, the current pastor of South Congregational Church in Rochester. The Rev. Capron wrote in his letter of resignation to South Congregational Church that he looked forward to "the unique privilege in molding the life of the new church organization."

A reception was given for Rev. and Mrs. Capron who were housed temporarily on Titus Avenue by Mr. Joseph Rayton until the building committee could provide a permanent parsonage. A site on Hudson Avenue was purchased and a building was erected.

His duties were many and he took each one to heart.

Two innovations made by The Rev. Capron were happily received by his congregation and achieved considerable success: the neighborhood mid-week prayer meetings and the institution of birthday letters, which were written by the pastor to all whose names had been placed on a list of contributors to the Parsonage Fund.  Sometimes Rev. Capron had to write a letter a day to further this project, which expanded his friendship with church members while helping to net a tidy sum for debt reduction.

The First Parsonage

The fund raising continued with new ideas of which some would become yearly traditions.  It was in June of 1911 that a first Strawberry social was held with Mrs. Heffer's class as the committee sponsoring the event.  Mrs. Muxworthy served as the chairman. Then in July a rubber social was held by the WCTU where old rubber was gathered and taken to a place that gave $50.00 in cash for the rubber.

Along with the fund raising many items were donated by the classes.  There was the lectern given by Mrs. Metcalf's class, and tablecloths for the dining room.  Mrs. Titus's class gave water pitchers and glasses for the pulpit.  Mrs. Estall Stanton's class furnished draperies for the altar rail, and the list went on.

## WCTU Gives The Church A Gift

Of all the developments in 1911, the most admirable was the presentation of the building by the WCTU as a gift to the newly formed church. The documentation of this gift transfer was done in a professional manner, and the proper signatures obtained on the original documents to this day are part of the historical archives of the church.

The original documents are old and very fragile. Therefore, they have been copied into this book, allowing everyone the opportunity to read the contents of such a gracious gift.

LAW OFFICES OF
EDNOR A. MARSH
Rochester, N.Y.

**Deed.**
Warranty.

Irondequoit Women's
Christian Temperance Union,

To

United Congregational
Church of Irondequoit.

Dated_______________19

**State of New York**

Monroe________________County ss.

Recorded on the 27th________________ day of November________1911, at 12:25____ o'clock ___p.m., in book No. 868___ of Deeds, at page 145___ and examined.

_____________James L. Hotchkiss
Clerk.

Williamson Law Book Co, Publishers, Rochester, N.Y.

**State of New York.**
County of        Monroe
City of        Rochester

On this 21st day of November in the year One thousand nine hundred and eleven before me, the subscriber, personally appeared Dora B. Titus to me personally known, who being duly sworn did depose and say that she is the President of the Irondequoit Women's Christian Temperance Union, the corporation described in and which executed the foregoing instrument, and resides in Irondequoit, N.Y.; that the said corporation has no corporate seal and that she signed and executed the said instrument by order of the Board of Directors of said corporation.

Ednor Marsh

Notary Public

THIS INSTRUMENT made this 20th day of November, 1911, between George H. Rudman, individually and as superintendant of the Union Sabbath School of Irondequoit, an unincorporated association, and Edward Rayner, as secretary of said Union Sabbath School, Chester A. Stanton, as treasurer thereof and all the aforesaid as Trustees for said Union Sabbath School of Irondequoit, and the United congregational Church, of Irondequoit, N.Y., a membership corporation successor in interest to said Union Sabbath School, and Sarah E. Howard, as administratrix of William Howard, deceased, parties of the first part, and the Irondequoit Women's Christian Temperance Union, of Irondequoit, N.Y., parties of the second part, WITNESSETH:

THAT whereas, heretofore and on or about the 18th day of March, 1885, said party of the second part did, by an instrument in writing, dated on that day and recorded in Monroe County Clerk's Office on March 21st, 1885, in Liber 392 of deeds at page 93, lease to George H. Rudman, superintendant, and William Howard, secretary and treasurer, of the Union Sabbath School of Irondequoit, and their successors in office, as trustees for said Union Sabbath School, premises in the Town of Irondequoit, being a part of lot 15 in Township 14, 7th range, containing one-half an acre of land and particularly described in said lease and in the deed of said premises to said party of the second part recorded in said Clerk's Office in Liber 387 of Deeds at page 162; and

WHEREAS, The said Union Sabbath School of Irondequoit has become merged and incorporated into the United Congregational Church of Irondequoit, N.Y., a religious corporation, one of the parties of the first part; and

WHEREAS, The said Church has upon concurring vote of at least two-thirds of the whole number of its directors ordered the cancellation of said lease; and

WHEREAS, The Supreme Court has by order duly granted, and entered in Monroe County Clerk's Office on the 20th day of November, 1911, given leave to said Church Corporation to make this release.

NOW, In consideration of one dollar and other good and valuable consideration to said parties of the first part duly paid, the receipt whereof is hereby acknowledged, said parties of the first part do hereby each and severally cancel and discharge said lease above described and release, convey and forever quit claim unto the said Irondequoit Women's Christian Temperance Union, party of the second part, all the right, title and interest of said parties of the first part, leasehold or otherwise, in and to said premises and each and every part thereof, and all the Estate and benefits of the said parties of the first part and each of them in and to the same, to the said party of the second part, its successors and assigns, to have and to hold the same forever.

IN WITNESS whereof said parties of the first part have hereunto set their hands and seals the day and year first above written.

       _George H. Rudman_________ (L. S. )

       _Edward Rayner_________ (L. S. )

       _C. A. Stanton_________ (L. S. )

       _________________ (L. S. )
Individually and as officers and Trustees of the Union Sabbath School of Irondequoit, N.Y.
The United Congregational Church of Irondequoit.
By  _H. E. Sherman_________
                          Clerk.

_Sarah E. Howard_________
As administratrix of William Howard.

State of New York)
County of Monroe ) ss

On this 21st day of November, 1911, before me personally appeared George H. Rudman, Edward Rayner and Chester A. Stanton

***

Warranty Deed (383)    Williamson Law Book Co., Publishers, Rochester, N.Y. 4-09

This Indenture,

Made the 21st day of November in the year One Thousand nine hundred and eleven

**Between** Irondequoit Women's Christian Temperance Union, a corporation of Irondequoit, N.Y., party of the first part, and United Congregational Church of Irondequoit, party of the second part,

**Witnesseth**, That the said party of the first part, in consideration of the sum of one dollar and upward ($1.00), lawful money of the United States paid by the said party of the second part, does hereby grant and release unto the said party of the second part, its successors, and assigns forever.

ALL THAT TRACT OR PARCEL OF LAND, situated in the Town of Irondequoit, Monroe County, New York, being part of lot #15 in Township #14, 7th range, bounded and descried as follows: viz? Commencing at a point in the center of the highway running east and west known as the Stanton Road; 2 chains 29 links, west from the southeast corner of aforesaid lot #15; thence north on a line parallel with the east line of the aforesaid lot #15, 2 chains 19 links; thence west on a line parallel with the south line of said lot #15, 2 chains 29 links; thence south on a line parallel with the east line of said lot #15; 2 chains 19 links to the center of the aforesaid Road known as Stanton Road; thence east along the center line of said Road and the south line of said lot #15, 2 chains 29 links to the place of beginning. Containing one-half acre of land and no more. The above descried Real Estate and premises being half and acre of land taken from the Real property owned by Charles Howard and adjoining on west the premises conveyed by Alfred P. Curtice and wife to School District #3.

STATE OF NEW YORK, )

COUNTY OF MONROE, )SS.

TOWN OF IRONDEQUOIT. )

We, the undersigned, being respectively the residing officer and the two inspectors of election hereinafter descried and all being members and deacons of the church hereinafter mentioned, do hereby certify as follows: that notice of a meeting of the "United Congregational Church of Irondequoit, N. Y.", to be held at the church on Titus Avenue in said Town on the evening of February 23, 1911 for the purpose of incorporating said church and for the election of six trustees thereof, was publicly given by Reuben A. Dake, the presiding officer of said church, by reading and stating the same from the pulpit to the congregation, for two concessive Sabbaths preceding the day of election, and at lest 15 days before the day of such election. That in pursuance of such notice, to wit, on the evening of February 22, 1911, and at the said church, the place where said church stately attend for divine worship, the people having assembled, the said Reuben A. Dake, presiding officer of such church, called the meeting to order, and duly adjourned until the evening of March first, 1911 at the same time and place. That on said adjourned evening, to wit, March first, 1911 at said time and place, the people having assembled, the said Reuben A Dake, called the meeting to order, stated the object of the meeting and called for nominations of two deacons of said church to preside at such election and to act as inspectors thereof, to receive the votes cast, to judge of the qualifications of electors and to return the names of persons duly chosen as trustees of said church.  That thereupon, the undersigned, James Howard and Frank E. Heffer, deacons of said church were duly elected by a majority of the embers of said church then present to preside at and act as inspectors of such election and to make return thereof,

That such meeting having been thus organized, it was moved and carried to proceed to the election of six trustees of said church. That thereupon, the ballots of persons entitled to vote at such election were duly cast; and the following are the names. Of the persons duly chosen by plurality of the ballots so cast to serve as trustees of the United Congregational Church of Irondequoit, N. Y,, and the terms of office for which they were respectively elected:  Seymour Titus and Almond J. Warrant, to hold office until the first annual election of trustees; James Pammenter and John Heffer to hold office until the second annual election of trustees; Abram Franke and Thomas B. Pengelly to hold office until the third annual election of trustees; and we further certify that at the said election and by the like plurality of votes cast, that it was duly decided that the said trustees and their successors should forever hereafter be called and known by the name and title of the "United Congregational Church of Irondequoit, N.Y.", and that said town of Irondequoit, Monroe County, N. Y., should e its principal place of worship.

In witness whereof, we, the presiding officers of said church and the two inspectors of election, duly elected to preside over said election have hereunto set our hands and seals this day of March, 1911.

Reuben A. Dake                                                                (L. S.)

James Howard                                                                  (L. S.)

Frank E. Heffer                                                               (L. S.)

STATE OF NEW YORK,                                                            )

COUNTY OF MONROE,                                                             )SS.

TOWN OF IRONDEQUOIT.  )

On this 3rd day of March, 1911, before me, the subscriber, personally appeared, Reuben A. Dake, James Howard, and Frank E. Heffer to me known to be the same persons who executed the foregoing certificate and they severally acknowledge to me that they executed the same.

Stephen A. Warren

Justice of the Peace

***

By 1912 the church was in full swing and reaching out to the community. Around this time, a Boy Scout troop was organized by Mr. Henry Sherman with Mr. Hunt taking the post as the first Scoutmaster. Notably, this was just two years after the founding of Boy Scouting in America.

With all the gains, there were some down sides. Around this time the big Bible that belonged to the Church was stolen along with some mugs and dishes from the dining room and thirty cents from the primary department. The stolen money was reported to the police and Sheriff Hammell was presented with the case. Upon hearing of the stolen Bible, Sheriff Hammell donated a new one in honor of his wife who was a Congregationalist.

It was the original idea of the Sunday School to start what they called "the Giving Christmas." For this project, each class decided what they would do and kept it a secret until the time of the Sunday school Christmas party. Some of the ideas that came out of this venture were the giving of dolls to hospitals, the making of aprons for the Industrial School, preparation of food baskets, and contributing bedding and clothing to needy families.

By 1913 money went to support the work of the Rev. H. E. Hazen at Madura, India. Rev. Hazen had visited the church that April to outline special missionary needs. Then in August of 1914, Mrs. H A. Hagaman passed away after providing sixty-four years of help to the Sunday school in Irondequoit. A mark of her successful efforts occurred a month later on Rally Day[6] when 335 students participated in

---

[6] Rally Day is observed in some congregations to celebrate a new start or a renewed effort in involving children, youth, and adults in Sunday morning

the Sunday school processional, which was ten times that of the original enrollment of the first little Sabbath School.

In 1915 a librarian and an assistant librarian were added as officers of the Sabbath School to keep track of the distribution of hymn books, scripts and petition books.  That year there were 490 in attendance on Children's Day.

The church and Sunday school were successfully moving forward through everyone's hard work, so in the summer of 1916, when Rev. Capron chose to accept a call to Bangor Maine, they took it in stride and formed a committee to find a new minister. His resignation letter follows:

> *"United Church is now in good condition to leave -- our attendance is good, our treasury is well-supplied -- our benevolences reasonably well-supported.  Although the effectiveness of a church is not always measured by the number on the roll, you have made a net gain of over a hundred members (since 1911).  You have made real progress in Christian living and in Christian service.  I urge you to take up with renewed energy the tasks of the church and to strive more than ever to deserve the name which you bear -- UNITED."*

It seemed strange, though, when on his departure, Rev. Capron's would warn the  Sunday: "Please don't tell the new pastor that comes that you wish to do things a certain way because you always have."  Later those parting words would become clear.

---

classes for Christian education. Rally Day may coincide with Promotion Sunday, but it may be observed at a different time. When Rally Day is observed on its own, focus on efforts to involve as much of the congregation as possible in Sunday school or other Christian formation opportunities.

# Rev. William J. Prout (1917-1925)

In 1916 the Rev. William J. Prout became pastor, and during his tenure plans for the present beautiful structure designed to be a landmark were in development. His pastoral duties were interrupted by the war, when he was called to serve as a chaplain. During his absence, the Rev. Robert McCaul and Rev. Charles R. Osborne served as pastors.

*** 

World War I began on July 28, 1914, when Austria-Hungary declared war on Serbia.

## Many Called To Serve

This seemingly small conflict between two countries spread rapidly; soon Germany, Russia, Great Britain and France were all drawn into the war, largely because they were involved in treaties that obligated them to defend certain other nations. Western and eastern fronts quickly opened along the borders of Germany and Austria-

Hungary.  Despite the stalemate on both fronts in Europe, two
important developments in the war occurred in 1917. In early April, the
United States, angered by attacks upon its ships in the Atlantic,
declared war on Germany, and twenty-two members of the United
Congregational Church answered the call for service in the Armed
Forces.

On the home front, the church building campaign continued. In
the summer of 1917, at a meeting held in the home of Mrs. E. Hickson,
the Dorcas Sabbath school class started the first building fund of $100
for the cornerstone for the new church.  Other classes of the Sunday
school and the Women's Guild contributed generously.

In March of 1917 the first Missionary Sunday was held.  With
its success came a desire to have our very own Missionary and funds
from the classes came pouring in.  The sum pledged on that day
amounted to $658.00 and by the close of the last quarter of the year, the
entire sum that was needed had been raised.

**Mr. & Mrs. Prout, Mr. Prouts Mother And Their
Nephew John Hadley Prout**

The war ended in the late fall of 1918, after the member
countries of the Central Powers signed armistice agreements one by
one and Rev. Prout resumed his duties and church continued to prosper.
Missions pledges for Missionary Sunday that were paid by the classes
totaled more than $900 in each of three successive years and the church

enlisted Rev. and Mrs. Giles Brown as special missionaries of the church.

* * *

The ratification of the Eighteenth Amendment in 1918 was the culmination of a seventy-year struggle to make temperance the nation's policy. The success of the Anti-Saloon League and the Women's Christian Temperance Union in getting a national prohibition law enacted, however, was undermined in New York State where the desire for local control of the alcohol trade ran contrary to the tenets of federal prohibition. New York State's attempt to rescind its ratification of the Eighteenth Amendment via a referendum, the passage of a law allowing for the sale of 2.75 beer and light wine, and repeal of the state's prohibition law posed a serious challenge to state and federal dry advocates.

Hard as it is to believe, World War I claimed an estimated 16 million lives while the influenza epidemic that swept the world in 1918 killed an estimated 50 million people. One fifth of the world's population was attacked by this deadly virus and within months, it had killed more people than any other illness in recorded history.

The plague had two phases. The first phase, known as the "three-day fever," appeared without warning. Few deaths were reported. Victims recovered after a few days. When the disease surfaced again that fall, it was far more severe. Scientists, doctors, and health officials could not identify this disease which was striking so fast and so viciously, eluding treatment and defying control. Some victims died within hours of their first symptoms. Others succumbed after a few days; their lungs filled with fluid and they suffocated to death. Those who survived knew how lucky they had been.

In 1919 Reuben A. Dake, "father" of the United Church, died at the age of seventy-five. He had served the Sabbath school and church for forty-three years; recognition of his community involvement was shown by naming the school after him.

At the fall congregational meeting in 1919, the church members were determined to raise money to complete payment of their current building debt and to consider a cash purchase for a lot on Titus Avenue adjacent to the church property on the west at a cost of $1700. The parsonage on the east side of Hudson Avenue was paid off five years prior to the purchase of the new lot.  By the end of the year, changes were in the wind.

***

It was written in the Plattsburgh Daily Republican, 17 January 1920, p. 1.

"On a cold winter's night a few…railroad men, detectives and express men who were at the Delaware and Hudson railway station had…a fleeting glimpse of the last shipment of 'wet goods' into Canada…   National prohibition had come to northern New York. The quiet, rural nights on the Canadian-New York border had come to an end and the lonely sound of the express train would soon be replaced by the sound of the bootlegger's speeding car and the pursuit of enforcement agents trying to stem the flood of illegal alcohol".

Liquor smuggling during national prohibition had become the stuff of legends. The failure of enforcement officials to eradicate bootlegging, the growth of an underground economy in conjunction with popular support of local smugglers, and the desire to maintain local control of enforcement of prohibition in northern New York suggest a correlation between local factors and the failure of national prohibition.  It seemed that the small group of women who had fought so hard for abstinence had to face the changing world.

Customs still held strong in some areas and would not change. As was the custom in these early days, marriages in church families usually took place in their homes, at the parsonage or in the city churches with which the families had long been connected, so it was a notable occasion when the wedding and reception of Lucy Hess and Elmer Pammenter on December 2, 1920 was held at the United Church. Dr. Pammenter's mother had been an active member and officer of the WCTU for many years, and his father, James Pammenter, was a member of the first Board of Trustees.

***

The church was doing well as a result of a supportive congregation.  Finances were at an all time high so at the 1921 annual meeting of the church, Rev.. Prout was presented with an automobile, and in 1925 the church voted to replace this car with a new one. When Rev. Prout resigned four months later, the Trustees were instructed to include the automobile as his parting gift.

# A Need To Expand The Church

The war over, in 1921 a committee was formed to look into the building of a new church. A meeting was called by the Trustees of the church at the request of the church ladies to discuss the question of a new building. The Building Committee consisted of J. Bristol (Chairman), George Hunt, George West, Frederick V. Metcalfe and Almond J. Warren, and the final vote was for the construction of a new church auditorium.

On March 11, 1921 the Dorcas class project was the presentation of the Mother Goose Pageant, which presented Mother Goose Rhymes. The pageant book was supported by the inclusion of thirty advertisements from local businesses, which demonstrated that the church was indeed feeling the golden age. Of the advertisements, one that stood out among the rest appeared at the bottom of the back of the program and was supplied by Rochester Gas & Electric Company. At this time, the United Congregational Church of Irondequoit was in the midst of its new church building campaign. A flyer of songs for the new church building campaign was printed, the cover song being "Irondequoit, the Beautiful."

## IRONDEQUIOT, THE BEAUTIFUL

(Tune 239, S. S. Hymnal)
O Beautiful for orchards fair
With Autumn's fruitful yield,
For gardens tilled with labor rare
And bright as emerald field
Irondequoit—Irondequoit, God bless our church Campaign
And give success to earnestness That we our goal may gain.
O Beautiful for homes made light
With Christian virtues fair
For parents trust in God and right
For children too who share
Irondequoit—Irondequoit. We'll ne'er these gifts despise

Let's not withhold, but give our gold,
To build for God let's rise.
O Beautiful for all that we
And Nature doth supply
Save one—a church of dignity
And fit for worship high
Irondequoit—Irondequoit, We long a Church to see
Let's rise and build, with ardor filled
And soon there such shall be.


It was in 1922 that the Rudman class organized a contest which proved very successful.  The class divided into two groups and called themselves the "Publicans" and the "Sinners".  Each group was presented with the responsibility to bring in new members to the class and they met the challenge with fervor.  The "Publicans" led the race at first and the "Sinners "worked harder to take the lead.  The contest continued until the classroom was filled to capacity. The contest reached its peak on Palm Sunday when 119 new members were presented with the "Sinners" in the lead.  The contest closed on Easter Sunday and the "Sinners "were deemed the winners with 17 more new members than the "Publicans".

In 1923 George H. Rudman died.  Mr. Rudman had served thirty-seven years as the Sabbath School superintendent, his name continued to live on as his family members became staunch members of the United Church and contributed greatly to its progress.

After four years of study, the Building committee was authorized by a unanimous vote at the 1925 annual meeting to proceed with the building of a new church. This committee was empowered to mortgage the land and building for up to $50,000.00. At the Annual meeting of the church on January 7, 1925, this resolution was adopted by unanimous vote:  "Resolved that the Building Committee chosen in 1921 be authorized to complete the plans and to proceed with the building of the church, that they be empowered to proceed with the collection of pledges for this purpose, and to take the necessary steps to mortgage the church land and buildings for an amount not exceeding $50,000." The congregation immediately conducted a building fund that raised 208 pledges totaling $74,000.00.

The design of the church was attributed to the Rev. William Prout, who chose the architectural design that combined features of several New England churches of the 1780 era, including the exterior, the balcony, the white trim, the use of tinted but not leaded window glass, and the Christopher Wren tower. Wren is best known as the architect for St Paul's Cathedral.  It was his third design that would form the basis for the plans for the Cathedral, but Wren modified them as the work progressed over a period of 35 years.  His tower design was renown.

The Trustees and the chairman of the Building Committee signed the necessary bonds to secure the mortgage for $50,000 from the Monroe County Savings Bank. On the Board of Trustees were Frederick V. Metcalfe, George Hallauer, Frank Tarrant, Raymond C. Howard, Louis Tietenburg, James Porter, Seymour Titus, Almond J. Warren and George West.  In the midst of the building project, in May of 1925, Rev. Prout resigned his post at the United Church to accept a call to Potsdam, New York.  The building would proceed with the chosen design.

Large amounts of Building Fund pledges were being paid and work was progressing, and in early 1926 the committee was authorized to obtain a second mortgage of $10,000.00 to finish the job. To secure this additional money, nine members of the Board of Trustees personally signed a bond making themselves liable should the church fail. These men were George Hallauer, Raymond Howard, Fred Metcalfe, James Porter, Louis Teitenburg, Frank Tarrant, Seymour Titus, Almond Warren, Albert Bristol and George West.

***

The church continued on its upward climb when on October 7, 1926 *"The Community Columns,"* a newspaper of the United Congregational Church, was born, and the first page of this four-page edition is as shown here

The Building Fund received the support of the full church in so many ways, with unique ideas for fundraising. One project done by the Dorcas class was the presentation of the tiny pocketed apron that came with the following poem:

. This neat little apron is sent to you,
And this is what we wish you'd do:
The little pocket you plainly see,
For a special purpose is meant to be.
Now measure your waistline inch by inch,
And see that the measure does not pinch,
For each small inch you measure round,
In the pocket put a penny sound.
The game is fair, you will admit,
You "waste" your money: we "pocket" it.
Please bring this apron on the appointed day,
And on the table your offering lay.
June 8 is the day we've set,
But just the same should the day be wet,
If not able to be present, dear friend,

The apron and money we hope you'll send.

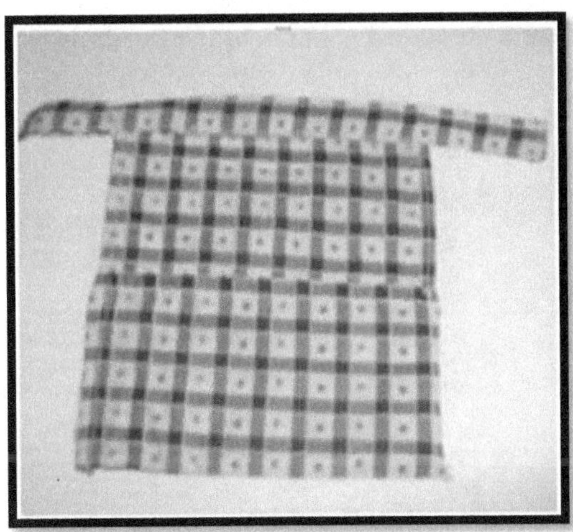

There was an extra apron and a note pointed out, *"The extra apron is for a friend or relative."* It was signed the Dorcas Class – United Congregational Church.

The Framing Of The Congregational Church Addition

Construction work was shaping up rapidly. The roof and tower were almost finished by October of 1926. The architects, Foot and Carpenter, were assured by the contractor in charge of the finishing work on the inside of the building that he would call in more men if needed.

1926 IUCC Cornerstone

# Rev. Charles S. Bergner (1925-1942)

**The Rev. Charles Bergner**

In 1927, completion of the plan for the church was left to the new pastor, the Rev. Charles S. Bergner, who was called to the post in 1925. In February, two years later, while a bitter blizzard raged outside, a week's ceremonies began in which the new structure was dedicated. Snow plowing practices in horse car days with their open front platforms, provided no protection for the driver whatever. He had to stand out on the platform in the weather." The early snow- equipment was primitive but effective. The greatest Rochester-area snow storm of the trolley era, which took place on January 29 and 30, 1925, tested all this equipment to its maximum extent. Most fortunately, a rebuilding of numerous snow fighting cars had been undertaken in 1923, so the fleet was really in top condition.

Snow began to fall in Rochester early on Thursday afternoon January 29th. What had appeared to be just another of the season's storms heightened its intensity by 4 o'clock that afternoon, just as the evening rush hour was beginning. The havoc of the storm wrecked plans to obtain the men who normally crewed the snow plows and sweepers as they were on tripper cars for that afternoon's rush hour traffic. Many automobiles were stalled directly on the streetcar tracks by the heavy snow, forcing city cars to slow down or stop. This prevented the timely return of crews to the car houses for reassignment to snow fighting equipment. Thus delayed, the Rochester city sweepers and plows got a late start on the storm. The heavy snows were so deep that pushers were required to keep plows moving through the mountainous drifts, and as many as five cars were put together in a single train for this purpose. High spots of the week were the sixteenth anniversary dinner and the address by Dr. S. Parks Cadman, president of the Federal Council of Churches of Christ in America.

## Dedication Service For the New Church Addition

The service of dedication was one of pride. A symbol of the United Congregational Church, was the unusual colonial architecture of the red brick church building. With its tall white columns in front and the belfry on the roof, the structure appeared more like a town hall or community center than a religious building. Dedication services were held with appreciation given to Mr. Charles Carpenter of Foote and Carpenter, the architects who were responsible for the beautiful Georgian Church.  Thanks were also given to the contractors and workmen who shared their skills. Much was said about the history of the church, which showed its community nature since its beginning in 1850, eleven years after the establishment of Irondequoit Township.

The week long dedication service would bring Congregational and other religious denominations into the church to celebrate the birth of the new structure to the church.  To close the celebration, Rev. Bergner said, "*As we dedicate our new church, pray for God's blessing on it.  If God's blessing is here, Irondequoit shall see a more consecrated life and The Kingdom will be nearer.*"

## Dedication Services For The Church Organ

A series of dedication services took place from February to March of 1927: the formal dedication of the new building, a service of dedication for the work of religious education and a banquet and service of fellowship for the young people. The ceremonies closed with a sixteenth anniversary banquet at which Mr. Bergner said, "*As we*

**The Sanctuary Completed**

In April the new organ was dedicated, with Professor George
E. Fisher as the organist.

Later, on April 24, 1927, the church held a full service entitled
"Dedication Services of the Church Organ," to give thanks to the Hook
and Hastings Organ Company for the organ they had provided. In its
day, Hook was the premier organ building company in the United
States.  The Hook brothers were sons of a cabinet maker in Salem,
Massachusetts. They apprenticed with the organ builder William
Goodrich.

The Hook firm built over 2,000 pipe organs, many of which are
still extant today and some remain in unaltered, original condition.
Appreciation during this service extended to Mrs. Arseneth Rogers and
Mr. and Mrs. George Hunt for the Aeolian Harp and Degan chimes,
and to Mr. Fred Metcalfe for the Doppel Flute.

These stops added greatly to the beauty and expressiveness of
the organ. Separate thanks were given to Prof. George E. Fisher, who

gave of his time and talent. Mr. Fisher played the organ at the Dedication Concert on March 25, 1927. Paul Benz, who was generally acknowledged to be one of the greatest organ voicers in the country, voiced the organ. Mr. Benz told Mr. Fisher that he thought this organ had the most beautiful tuba he had ever voiced. On Sunday, February 27, 1927 at the 10:30 a.m. service, the presentation of the keys of the church was held along with the acceptance of the keys by the church. An evening music service followed the presentation of the keys, and then on Monday, February 28 at 8:00 a.m., a Fellowship for Young People was held.

The celebration continued to Wednesday, March 2 at 8:00 a.m., when an Inter-church Fellowship was held, and then on Friday, March 4 at 7:00 p.m., the Sixteenth Anniversary Banquet was held.

## Purchasing The Cornerstone

This was a banner year for the United Congregational Church of Irondequoit when they raised the money to buy the cornerstone. On May 30 at 3:30 p.m., the Laying of the Cornerstone service was held. At the service, Miss Leone Titus did the reading of the contents of the corner stone, and the Chairman of the Building Committee, Albert J. Bristol, and the Rev. Charles S. Bergner placed the cornerstone. Rev. Walter H. Rollins, Secretary of the Congregational Churches of New York State, preached the dedication sermon. The dedication service for the cornerstone was finally held on February 27, 1927.

The Rev. Rollins stated,

"It is a sacred task to erect an edifice where men may come to worship God. The labors of men who make such a building possible are the symbols of community service and of their partnership with God. In such a structure the material things are blended with the spiritual things of life into a building which men may see and a holy place where they feel God to dwell.

When we read as much that is unpleasant concerning religion, we may ask why it is necessary to construct a new church building. Many persons say the church and religion are decaying. They said the same thing years ago and still the church grows. In the seventies, ministers predicted the bicycle was the one thing which would drive the church out of existence. Today one scarcely sees a bicycle on Sunday.

In the same measure they speak of radio and moving pictures. These things will not supplant the church.

The church has been victor in every generation because the hearts of men cannot be satisfied by merely material entitles. Learning and education of themselves will not ring satisfaction. The soul of man demands those things which the world cannot give.

After the World war men said frankly that they had lost interest in religion, but during the last few years they have been coming more and more interested in the church. The material things have not satisfied them. The first symbol of this building constructed of brinks and stones and steel is that it is a place of meeting, a place of worship God."

The Rev. N. Courtenay James, minister of the Sea Breeze Congregational Church, offered a prayer. James M. Ropes of the South Congregational Church spoke for the organization, and the Rev. Charles E. Berger was present.

The new church presented new challenges. When the Sunday school classes moved into the remodeled rooms, the Primary Department was divided with a new class for children under five years of age. This new class was to be called Kindergarten[7].

But not all things changed. Thousands of summer visitors flocked to the resorts on Lake Ontario and Irondequoit bay.  At the mouth of the bay was the famous resort of Sea Breeze with hotels and amusement rides.  On the shores of the Bay, at least a dozen hotels at one time or the other offered meals, rooms, boats, fishing tackle and, like the Glen Haven, elaborate accommodations of the resort variety. The Newport House, first built by Joseph Vinton as a sawmill, had served customers on the Bay since 1840.  The layout of the land made the  area become known as the "Coney Island of western New York". The custom of the Sunday school picnic being held at the Newport House on Irondequoit Bay, remained intact. The group would descend on Newport Hill in a canopy-topped buggy and feast beneath the

---

[7] The first kindergarten in the United States was founded in Watertown, Wisconsin by Margarethe (Margaret) Meyer Schurz (wife of activist/statesman Carl Schurz) in 1856. Kindergarten (German, literally means "children's garden") is a form of education for young children which serves as a transition from home to the commencement of more formal schooling. Children are taught to develop basic skills through creative play and social interaction.

willows. There was one change in the routine and that was the group took to gathering water lilies.

The Junior Department of the Sunday school was started under the leadership of Miss Cecilia McCutcheon. Along with the Rev. Mr. Wilkins, the Junior Department sold Jell-O to contribute to the Daily Vacation Bible School expenses and toward defraying the Sunday school expenses for their equipment.

A boys and girls club formed that fall holding regular meetings to make new dolls and toys and to repaint old ones to give to those less fortunate than themselves at Christmas time.

Generosity was seen from all corners as the church moved forward with the rest of the world. It was a great time in the church, town and country history. Briefly summarized, 1920s were a time of unbelievable prosperity. The stock market was going through the roof and the United States seemed to have the formula for limitless prosperity. However, the same formula that generated all of that profit would also be the cause of Black Tuesday.

***

Of course, few people in the mid-1920s could have foreseen such a disaster. After the postwar recession of 1920-21, American business seemed to have entered a golden age that would go on forever. New industries were booming—the automobile, radio, motion pictures, household appliances and much more, and the public was buying more than ever.

In reality, the economy was not quite as rosy as it appeared. While new industries were flourishing, some older and more basic ones, such as farming, mining, textiles and lumber, were suffering a steady decline in prices that gradually undermined the country's entire economic structure. Nevertheless, the sensation of prosperity was real enough and had an intoxicating effect on American morals and manners, giving rise to the frenetic era know as the Jazz Age.

In many ways, the economic and social trends of the decade were closely paralleled by the political climate. The Great War had been fought to make the world safe for democracy, and for a while it seemed to have worked. In the end, though, the promising political trends proved as fragile as the economic boom with which they coincided.

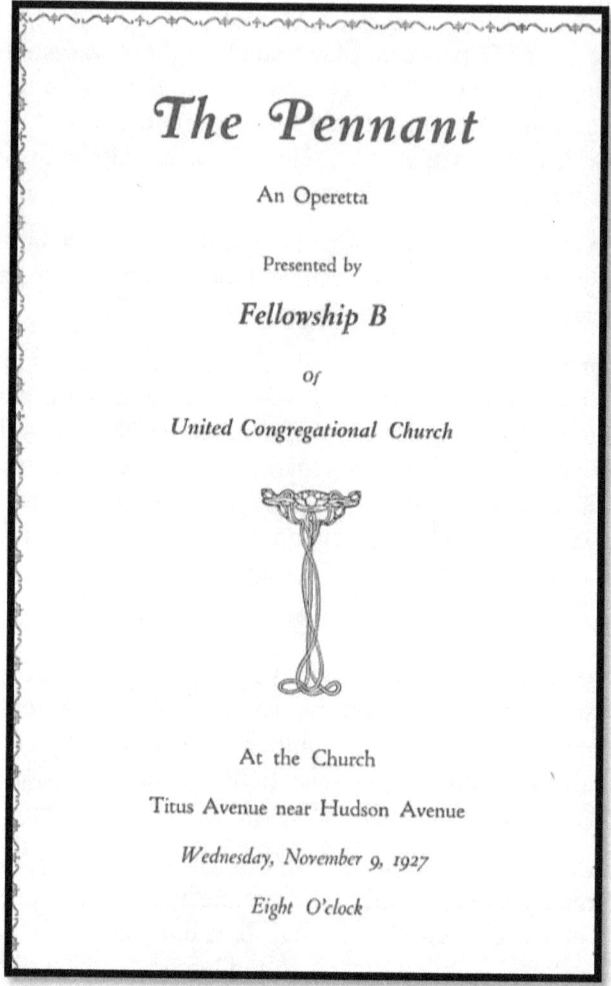



On November 9, 1927 the United Congregational Church offered hope to the community by the presentation of an operetta called "The Pennant," which was a well attended fundraiser for the Church Building Fund..

## Church Organizes Departments

By 1928 the church had five departments. The Membership Department kept the membership interested and busy while seeking to increase the membership. Their responsibilities also included advertising the church and directing the social life of the church.

The Educational Department provided the teaching and training of the youth and the church.  They sponsored all organizations for young people, including fellowships, Boy Scouts, Girl Scouts and D.V.B.S.

The Service Department was in charge of service to foreign missions, home missions, social service in Rochester and Irondequoit, and cooperation with all service organizations including WCTU, the Salvation Army and Near East Relief.

The Evangelistic Department managed the evangelistic work in the church, personal work and the assisting in the spiritual services in the church. This committee was made up of the Deacons of the church.

The Finance Department provided the budget, the current expense fund and the care of the property. This department included the Trustees and the Budget and Finance Committees.

The services of the church included the Sunday morning family worship at 10:30, the junior church after the children's sermon, and church school.  On Sunday evenings services were arranged according to the interest of all the church and the community. The first Sunday evening in each month was a program for high school age, the second Sunday evening for the benefit of the community, the third Sunday evening for the benefit of those of university age, and the last Sunday evening was devoted to music. Wednesday nights there were devotional services, the exception being the first Wednesday night during the six winter months when the Membership Committee conducted congregational dinners and entertainment.

By 1928 Herbert Hoover, Secretary of Commerce, was elected thirty-first President of the United States.  Prohibition was in full swing, which was important to church members as their history blended with the WCTU, who had hoped for prohibition all along, but this brought about new problems.

***

The crash of 1929 ended the seemingly infinite prosperity of the 1920s. Millionaires had become paupers overnight. Those who believe in the strength of the economic bubble and invested everything they had lost everything. Of course, the economy weakened and unemployment skyrocketed. The Great Depression had begun.

Under the Rev. Charles S. Bergner, the United Congregational Church continued to offer hope though the falling economy pushed hard showing an annual interest on church indebtedness exceeding the pastor's salary.  This was just a presage of things to come as the congregation of 450 began to face the reality of a national depression and economic stress period.

But the members did not give up as they again sought projects to raise funds.  From the "mile of pennies" to Rev. Bergner taking a cut in his already meager salary, to holding meetings in homes to save money on heating the church, the members continued their financial cutback crusade.

By 1933 John Thorne reported $7.00 on hand and a debt of $2054.00.  He wrote "We are determined through increased personal sacrifice that United Congregational Church shall go on." And it did!

## The Twenty-Fifth Anniversary Jubilee

In 1936 the United Congregational Church of Irondequoit, under the direction of Mrs. Polly Rogers Hunt, a charter member, celebrated its twenty-fifth anniversary with a candle-lighting service symbolizing the origin and development of the church. This would become a tradition for the future. The ceremony was further enhanced by an organ concert by Tom Grierson.

Beautiful ceremonies with blending to the current joy and gladness with fond recollections of those members of the congregation who had passed to their final reward marked the silver anniversary of the United Congregational Church. As a gift to show the church appreciation, the quilt shown here was made for the Rev. Bergner and his wife. It was made in 1936 by Mrs. Newman, a member of the Ruth Circle.

Quilt Made In 1936

Marking its silver anniversary on March 8, 1936 was a memorable day for the United Congregational Church. The Rev. Bergner and a committee were in charge and had set for the congregation to assemble early for the formal opening of the Jubilee at 11:00 a.m., at which time the 86th anniversary of Sabbath school work in the vicinity also was commemorated. The Rev. William J. Prout, of Potsdam, New York, a former pastor of the church, occupied the pulpit for the morning service to deliver his personal message. Rev. Prout recalled the names of several members who had passed away since his departure eleven years prior. Eyes were moist as he mentioned names of men and women active in the church, especially when he referred to "Uncle Jim" Howard and "the golden-voiced Eddie Raynor." He said that Raynor' voice was the most beautiful ever heard in this and many other churches, and would have thrilled thousands in theaters if Eddie had accepted one of the many operatic offers he had received.

Floral arrangements greeted the multitudes as they entered the church that Sunday morning. Mrs. Polly Rogers Hunt was put in charge of the birthday candle ceremony. Held at the afternoon services, a mammoth birthday cake was illuminated by twenty-five candles lit by members who had joined the church in each successive year. Mrs. Eva Rudman Sherman presented a historical sketch associated with the religious progress of the congregation, and a musical program by the adult and junior choirs followed.

Mrs. Rudman Sherman, who prefaced her history of the first twenty-five years with an anonymous verse, presented a talk on the church's history.

Silver bells in the tower of time
Ring out upon our way
To celebrate in joyous chime
Our Anniversary Day.
May their symphony foretell
The joys that life shall hold.
Until their melody shall swell
From bells of brightest gold.

At the outset as the WCTU, there were seventy-two active and eight associate members, and the membership grew rapidly.

L. To R:  Grace DeSmit, Marjorie Sherman, Gladys Metcalfe, Olivette Leake, Imogene Tyler, Mrs. John Daggs and Mildred Grant

The WCTU, which had its start in 1884, had celebrated its fiftieth anniversary two years earlier, in 1934, and shared group photos taken of those responsible for the growth of the WCTU. The members posed in the fashions of the late 1880s.

The Whole W.C.T.U. Founder's Group Wearing the Fashions Of The Late 1880s

***

The depression years proved to be a time of testing for the United Church. A second mortgage had to be added to cover the cost of annual church indebtedness. With hard times on every side, the forty-five United Church families found the going rough. Through the ongoing imaginative moneymaking schemes, the church managed to weather the depression years.

The 25th Anniversary of the church, celebrated in 1936 included a birthday candle lighting service. Mr. Prout returned to preach the sermon at the special service of remembrance and an impressive birthday candle-lighting ceremony was arranged by Mr. George Hunt. From two larger candles, symbolizing the early Sunday school and the W.C.T.U., twenty-five candles were lighted, each held by a person who had joined the church in successive years since 1911. In the afternoon an organ concert was presented by Tom Grierson, and a welcome was provided by Mrs. Nesbit Holland (the former Betty Dake, granddaughter of Reuben A. Dake). Mrs. Harry Sherman presented a review of the church history.

In the afternoon a historical and musical service included the presentation of a twenty-five-year history of the United Church that was prepared by Mrs. Harry Sherman.

Three weeks after the celebration, Mr. Bergner resigned as pastor of the church to join the U.S.O. Mr. Bergner died unexpectedly in May of 1960.

The Bonnie Blue Star Quilt that had been made to commemorate the twenty-fifth anniversary of the United Congregational Church in 1936 is embroidered with 629 names. Each person was required to pay at least ten cents for the privilege of having his or her name appear on it. The money went to the Church Building Fund. When the Rev. Bergner departed in 1942 to join the U.S.O. after seventeen years of service with the church, the quilt was presented to Mrs. Bergner.

She would return it to Irondequoit in 1961 so that it could be displayed again at the time of the church's fiftieth anniversary.

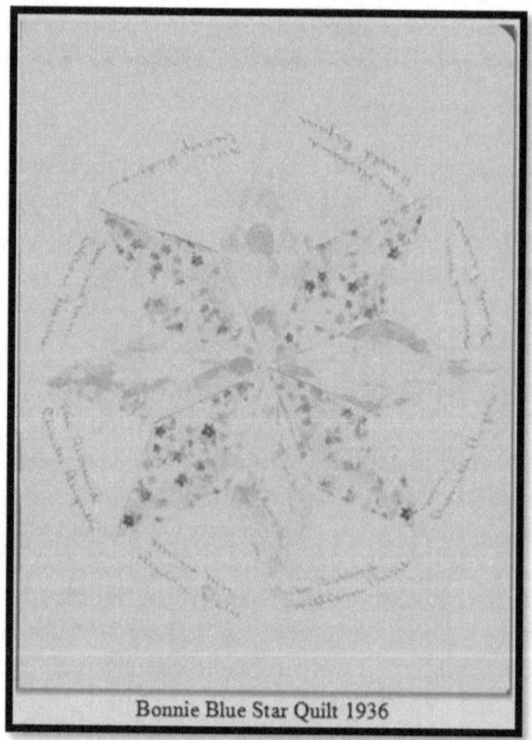

Bonnie Blue Star Quilt 1936

Mrs. Bergner requested that Mrs. Ruth MacGregor "act as custodian of the quilt as long as she could," as she was an active member of the Ruth Circle. All of the names were embroidered on the quilt by Mrs. MacGregor's mother, Mrs. George Newman.

***

World War II began on September 1, 1939, when Germany attacked Poland without a formal declaration of war. Ultimatums were issued to Hitler for the immediate withdrawal of German forces from Poland. When the deadlines expired, Great Britain and France declared war on Germany on September 2, 1939. Germany had Italy and Japan on its side and became known as the Axis powers.

Pearl Harbor, on the island of Oahu, Hawaii, was attacked by the Japanese Imperial Navy on December 7, 1941. The surprise attack was masterminded by Admiral Isoroku Yamamoto. On December 8, 1941 the United States—until then neutral in World War II—formally declared that a state of war existed between the United States and the Japanese empire. Some historians believe the United States presence helped change the Allies.

Up from the ashes of the depression rose office buildings, schools, factories, and dams in thousands of government sponsored work projects. New Deal agencies gave work to everyone, from road builders to artist and writers. That man in the White House, called such by the republicans was FDR and he was to do more to change the social structure of American than any president since Lincoln. As a result of the New Deal, labor unions became more powerful, farmers got government subsidies for the first time, and big business took a back seat.

Even today, after the end of World War II, assessing its total cost is difficult. Centuries of man's noblest, most deeply humane accomplishments in the arts and in learning were consumed in the flames.

The war reached out in all areas, including the church. The Congregational Church board of Trustees had approached the bank holding the mortgage in order to make a deal. The representative of the board of Trustees was told that if the church could make an offer for the entire mortgage, the bank would consider disposing of it at a ten-percent discount, which sounded reasonable, so the issue was presented to the Church Extension Society[8], which informed the trustees that the

---

[8] The Extension Society was incorporated on October 2,1946 as the Church Extension Society." Every Pastor and Lay Representative to the Annual Conference is an official member of the Society. Each year the members elect Officers and Directors who manage the Society's day-to-day business.

mortgage at the time was larger than they could handle, but that if it could be reduced to $25,000, they would consider it.

Two years later the trustees went back to the bank to ask for a commitment for the ten-percent reduction but found that the bank had taken the offer off the table.  The bank said that when they made their proposal, they felt the mortgage was weak, but it had since been reduced and the church was in such excellent financial condition that they thought the mortgage sound and were no longer willing to dispose of it at a discount.

***

In March of 1939, the Sabbath school started by the W.C.T.U. were in full swing of celebration for their Centennial year.  The preparation kept hands and minds busy as they worked toward making their 100 years a memorable landmark.  The Sabbath school had come a long way since its inception in 1839, prior to the organization of the church so it was only fitting for them to celebrate; really celebrate the event.

On that glorious Sunday morning, after the service there was a reception in the Sabbath school auditorium, and for that occasion, a poem was written and made part of the service. No name appears as the author.

**THE CHURCH AT THE CROSSING**

Out from the city with its noisy street
Out where the air is pure and sweet,
There at the crossing where two roads meet
Stands a country church.

Away from the rush, the jam and the show.
Back where the fragrant wild flowers grow
And songbirds nest in branches low
Is this country church.

Near to the grange, the school or the store.
A few simple houses say three or four
And a few great tress where once there were more
By the country church.

On the Sabbath day its bell will ring
And kindly folk will come and sing
The Praise of Him who peace did bring
To the country church.

"Faith of Our Fathers," or "Jesus Saves,"
Or, "Love Divine", which honest hearts crave.
The People sing and children behave
In the country church.

And when the last invitation is given,
And old-fashioned saints re gathered in heaven,
We'll meet with those whose sins were forgiven
Back in the country church.

It was a time to think about those who had organized the Sabbath School and the families who played major roles in helping to make it a reality. Remembrance was for those who where there and those who had passed and joy was found in knowing that their legacy lived on.

# Reaching Out For New Members

In an effort to bring more people to the church by letting them know they were welcomed, the United Congregational Church presented an Invitation to the Services during Lent of 1941. Lent was an exceptional way of extending their hand, as it is the forty-day liturgical season of fasting and prayer before Easter. The forty days represent the time Jesus spent in the desert, where, according to the Bible, he endured temptation by Satan. Different churches calculate the forty days differently, but the purpose remains the same.  Lent is the preparation of the believer—through prayer, penitence, almsgiving and self-denial.

On February 16, 1941 the invitations to join the United Congregational Church in celebrating Lent was sent to all religious denominations as part of the attendance invitation to the service held for Brotherhood Week.

The National Conference of Christians and Jews founded National Brotherhood Week in 1931 as a human relations organization dedicated to fighting bias, bigotry and racism in America. The invitation that was sent follows.

**TODAYS WORLD NEEDS A GOOD RELIGION**

Your Neighborhood church stands with its white columns, on a convenient corner, near your home, ready to welcome you to the fellowship in the service of God.  It endeavors to show forth the spirit and beauty of Christ in all seasons under all conditions of the world and mankind.

**COME AND WORSHIP WITH US**

United Congregational Church of Irondequoit is well equipped and established.

It has been in the community since 1851.  The present beautiful edifice was built in 1926.

**CHURCH GOING FAMILIES ARE HAPPIER FAMILES**

The children enjoy our Church School with its consecrated and capable teachers.  The Church School convenes at 10:00 o'clock every Sunday morning.  The children need their parents with them in the Church Worship Service at 11:00 a.m.  We will all need the uplift of worshipping together in faith and good will.

**THE LENTEN SEASONS IS JUST AHEAD**

The regular church services have a special attraction during Lent.

The church continued reaching out to the community and it was this effort that lead to an extraordinary event. On February 9, 1941 the first issue of *"The Irondequoit Churchman"* was born. This newspaper provided information about Irondequoit and points of interest. This first issue was widely accepted, so for the next twelve months it was printed for delivery on the first Sunday of the month with the following church ministers providing articles for the issues..:

The United Congregational Church, led by the Rev. Charles Bergner (Titus Avenue at Cooper Road)

Summerville Presbyterian Church, led by the Rev. Oscar Brownback (Stop 43, St. Paul Blvd.)

Lutheran Church of the Resurrection, led by the Rev. Eugene Stowell (St. Paul Blvd. at Cooper)

Seneca Methodist Church, led by the Rev. Reginald Cory (Schofield Road)

All Saints Episcopal Church, led by the Rev. Ernest K. Nicholson (Winona Blvd. at Chestnut Hill Drive).

This paper allowed each church an opportunity to become involved in activities being held in Irondequoit. Each issue showed improved content and layout design, and by December 1941, articles were contributed additionally by:

The Transfiguration Lutheran Church, led by the Rev. Howard A. Kuhnle (Culver Road at Avondale Road)

Durand Congregational Church, led by the Rev. Gerald E. Boyce (Culver Road)

Irondequoit Presbyterian Church, led by the Rev. Harry C. Benson (Culver Road near Ridge Road).

The four-page newspaper was now an eight-page spread.  The idea continued to grow and serve the community of Irondequoit.

# Rev. Lloyd R. Stamp (1943-1954)

The time was again upon the church for change, when the Rev. and Mrs. Bergner decided to move and the Rev. Bergner stepped down.

In the spring of 1943 the Rev. Lloyd R. Stamp was called as pastor of the United Congregational Church.  Rev Stamp was well qualified having thirteen years of teaching and campus ministries at Colgate and Syracuse Universities.  The church looked forward to the future with Rev. Stamp.

**Rev. Lloyd Stamp**

Rev. Stamp sent out a letter with a twofold purpose: first, a word of introduction as the new pastor and, second, a personal word of greeting to each member of the congregation.  Different from the past, this change was welcomed.  Having the pastor present himself in this way to the congregation was well received.

A pre-war building boom in Irondequoit brought many new families into the community, and church membership rose to 453 in 1943.  From the beginning the church had retained its interdenominational character and its emphasis on the Christian education of young people and the vitality of the dual traditions made the United Congregational Sunday School seem almost magnetically attractive to the growing community.

Rev. Stamp held two Vesper Communion Services and a Testimonial dinner in recognition of the returned veterans. An Honor Roll Committee that was established in 1942 included the Rev. Charles S. Bergner, Mr. J. Frederick Babcock, Mr. William Clarke, Mr. Earl G. Lawrence, Mrs. Blanche Woodworth, Mr. & Mrs. S. Lloyd Redfern, the Rev. Lloyd R. Stamp, Mr. William S. Thorne and Mr. Howard Tyler.  This was indeed an eventful year for all.  The Dorcas Class rededicated the dining room and made curtains for the windows.

Just as long standing and involved was the Berean Class and in 1944 the Berean Class celebrated 40 years as part of the Sabbath School.  A celebration was held at which the current teacher, Miss Maude West wrote and presented a history of the class.

Miss Maude West, preceptress at Irondequoit graduated from Geneseo normal school in 1902.  Some North American universities had a special student position called preceptor held by student volunteers who assist the staff professor and teaching assistants of a large lecture class by helping design certain lessons and holding their own office hours and review sessions. It was considered to be a good leadership experience.  Preceptor was the title of the day for student teaching assistants as well as a faculty member of which Miss Maude West seemed to be. at the time.

## Bausch And Lomb Make A Request

During World War II, Bausch and Lomb approached the Irondequoit Congregational Church for permission to install a lighted cross, on the church steeple; the church was the only building in the area that was the correct height and necessary distance from Bausch and Lomb, at St. Paul Blvd. and Smith Street, to calibrate the sights of the Norden bombsight.

The Norden bombsight was designed for use on U.S. Navy aircraft by Carl Norden, a Dutch engineer who emigrated to the United States in 1904 and worked on bombsights at the Sperry Corporation before starting his own company.  It contained the main operational portions of the bombsight and consisted primarily of three parts: a mechanical analog computer that calculated the impact point of the bombs relative to the aircraft as an angle, a small telescope used as the primary sight, and a system of electric motors and gyros that moved the telescope so a single point on the ground remained stationary in the sight. It was the lens that Bausch and Lomb was constructing and testing.

This proposition brought much controversy in the church since prior to the 1950s Congregational churches did not display a cross on their steeples and the purpose of the bombsight was objectionable to some. But the war had touched church families in many ways and eventually patriotism and the war effort prevailed. Today the lighted cross on the steeple is an integral part of the church building and the church history.

By 1943 the United Congregational Church of Irondequoit had reduced the mortgage debt from $45,750 to $17,000 and was calling out to its members to help take care of the balance. Admittedly no time was ideal for raising money, but the opinions of economists and shrewd businessmen supported the opinion of the Trustees to clear this debt. This was a time in history when the country was in the clutches of an inflationary period. *"With dollars cheap and plentiful they will not buy as much in repairs and maintenance as they will in paying off debts contracted when dollars were costly."*

At a meeting during 1947, the following revision was made to the Constitution and By-Laws of the United Congregational Church of Irondequoit.  Article VIII, Section 2, (3) was amended to read: *"The annual meeting of the church shall be held on the second Wednesday of January, at which time the annual reports shall be presented and officers elected, and such other business transacted as may be specified in the call or authorized in the By-Laws. This meeting shall be called by the Clerk in the manner specified in the paragraph next preceding. The fiscal year shall begin on January 1."*

There were two propositions to vote on to THE BASIS OF UNION. They were

"Resolved, that our church hereby register its decision upon the proposal to unite the Evangelical and Reformed Church and the Congregational Christian Churches into the United Church of Christ, in accordance with the Basis of Union dated 22 January 1947."

"Resolved, that in the event of the consummation of the union our church hereby undertakes to continue the same relations with the Congregational Church of Irondequoit that it now holds with the Fellowship of the Congregational Christian Churches."

Beginning on Sunday, April 18, 1948, pledges were taken at the morning service. Those who were unable to attend were called upon that afternoon by one of a team of visitors to receive the pledge. It was set that the pledges should be paid in full by July 1, 1949.

***

The war's end found the United States and the USSR the two greatest powers in the world.  By the time of the signing of the Axis satellite treaties early in 1947, the two countries were drawing apart. Friction over the treaties with Austria, Germany and Japan and Soviet aggressive designs in Eastern Europe brought increasing tension, and by the end of 1948 their relationship could be considered one of cold war. In 1950 armed conflict arose in Korea between Soviet-backed Communist forces and United Nations forces led by the United States. The cold war between the East and West continued thereafter, with the Communists striving for world domination through subversion and infiltration, and the West seeking to frustrate their designs.

***

In 1945 another change came to the way the church communicated with the congregation.  The *"United Church News"* was created with the first issue sent on September 1, 1945. The lead paragraph said, *"This is the first issue of a new venture in church publicity. Each month the "United Church News" will come to your home with announcements of activities, items of interest and important statements regarding the work Of the United Congregational Church."*

## The Flag Of 95 Stars

Early in the spring of 1942, several of the young men of the church entered the service of the country. Rev. Bergner, then pastor of the United Church, appointed a committee of three men and one woman to work with him in visiting each of the young men and women before they were called to leave. At these visits each was given the New Testament and a little Book of Prayers. They were also given a few words of spiritual advice along with the promise to keep them informed of the activities of their church at home.

They were remembered on their birthdays and Easter, and at Christmas they received a card and message along with a remembrance of one dollar. Early in November, at a Sunday morning worship service, a Service Flag with forty stars was dedicated.

No one was excluded from the changes that the war brought
about. The Irondequoit United Congregational Church saw over
twenty-two young men of the congregation entering the service. At the
end of World War II, ninety-five stars were on the service flag. There
were two gold stars, one for Robert Kippel and one for Raymond Pitts.
On March 3, 1946 at 4:00 p.m. the United Congregational Church held
a Service of Recognition for the members of the Honor Roll
representing those in active service as well as those soldiers who had
returned home

During this touching ceremony,  the members formed a semi-
circle at the front of the sanctuary. When all the candles were lit, the
congregation united in singing the closing hymn following the prayer
for those in service. The Hymn chosen on this occasion was "Eternal
Father, Strong to Save."

The flag would lay for years in the archives until Anne Smith
and her husband paid to have it framed.  The flag is now hanging in the
present Fellowship Room As the pastor read the names of those on the

Honor Roll in active service, the person designated by the family to light the candle came forward, received a candle, had it lit by the Pastor, and then returned to the foot of the chancel steps.

| THE HONOR ROLL | |
| --- | --- |
| **In Active Service** | |
| John C. Anderson | Robert C. Hughes |
| Robert Baart | Frederick Johnson |
| Jack B. Barrett | Richard Kaiser |
| Donald A. Bergner | Robert S. Kaiser |
| H. S. Bristol | Maynard D. Lee |
| Robert J. Burns | William A. List |
| Edward W. Clarke | James R. List |
| Peter D. Coutts | Samuel W. Lloyd Jr. |
| Hamilton I. Driggs | Donald MacGregor |
| Joyce Q. Flint | John F. Muxworthy, Jr |
| James R. Gohl | Henry B. Peters |
| Charles R. Graffrath | Robert Pollard |
| Howard F. Green | Richard H. Rippey |
| Melvin J. Hamann | Douglas W. Slater |
| Alfred C. Hamilton, Jr. | John A. Spry |
| Eugene Earl Hess | Edgar L. Stoddard |
| William Hogestyn | Roger W. Sherman |
| John Hogestyn | David C. Titus |
| Robert Potter | Barbara Van Lent |
| **Honorably Discharged** | |
| Robert Allan | George R. Kaiser |
| Ezra Armstrong | George M. Locke |
| Wakeman R. Auble, Jr. | Donald A. List |

| | |
|---|---|
| Walter J. Baird | John D. Locke |
| Wesley W. Bell | Allen E. Martin |
| Rev. Charles S. Bergner | Arthur McWade |
| Carl A. Brown | Robert Mulcock |
| Mildred A. Brown | Hiram A. Newman |
| Violet L. Canham | Theodore H. Peck |
| Roger Chapman | Robert M. Potteiger |
| Richard H. Chapman | Bruce W. Reamer |
| Percival John Clarke | Robert F. Revard |
| Stanley S. Clarke | W. T. Rudman |
| Royal C. Daggs | Richard Seymour |
| Robert P. Driggs | Edward G. Snider |
| Allen E. Dye | Charles W. Stanton |
| Robert W. Edwards | Paul D. Stanton |
| Barbara A. Foster | Edward E. Sundt |
| George H. Fritz | William Thorne |
| Robert V. Gianniny | Howard W. Tyler |
| Robert T. Graffrath | Jackson O. Vickers |
| Donald W. Grant | Dr. Duane Walker |
| Wesley McDonald Grant | Warren H. Walker |
| Albert S. Jerram | Kenneth Warren |
| Donald Alan Hess | Willard W. Warren |
| George E. Hughes, Jr. | Wesley C. Warren |
| Douglas P. Hunt | Robert F. Woodworth |
| **Killed in Action** | |
| Raymond F. Pitts | |
| William Robert Hoffman | |

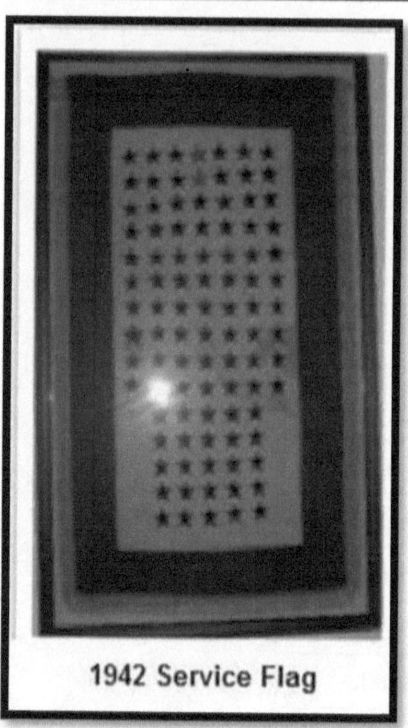

**1942 Service Flag**

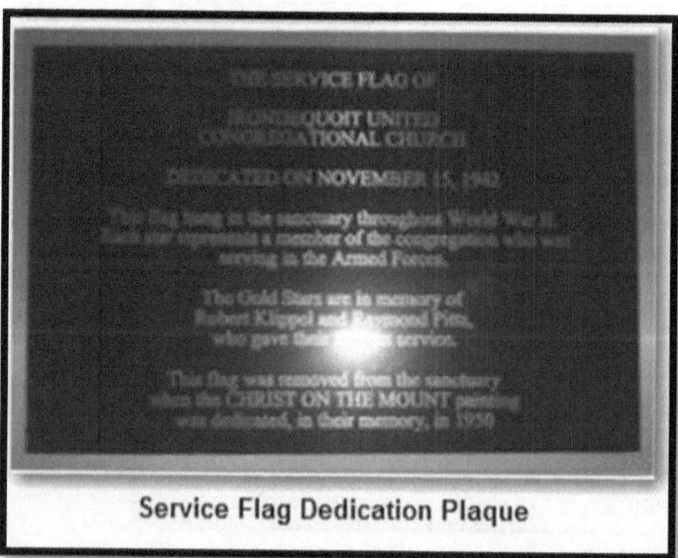



**Service Flag Dedication Plaque**

Between 1946 and 1947 the Women's Guild formed a lending library. For the library, members donated or loaned books, and the Guild also purchased some new books. The library was located in the church office, where 235 books accumulated.

So many changes were happening during this period that showed its growth and outreach. There was the Men's Club of the United Congregational Church that held monthly dinner meetings from October through May of the year. This group alone averaged eighty-five members during this period.

The work continued to finalize the church interior after the building addition was up. Participation by members was always prevalent and when it came to the finished building, there were many who stepped up. The women of the church, many of whom had labored in the "finishing", preserved another old tradition by giving money for hymnals, chairs, tables, curtains, and kitchenette equipment. They also undertook major renovating and remodeling projects in the church dining room and kitchen. All of this made the building ready for the ceremony that would be held next.

## The Burning Of The Mortgage

The day that the church looked forward to finally arrived. The canceled mortgage for the United Congregational Church was burned on Sunday night, October 23, 1949. More than four hundred people attended this special ceremony, in which a brief history of the church was presented, followed by a reception. At the ceremony the mortgage was lighted by George West, the treasurer of the Church Building Fund since 1924, and Mrs. George Hun, Daughter of Mrs. Asenath Rogers, the oldest charter member of the church.

In the sermon, Rev. Stamp pointed out that cancellation of the mortgage brought the congregation into unity with the past by completing the work of the church's founders. He said it was their duty to look to the future and meet the challenge of education of Christian youth and spread their influence in benevolent and missionary work.

The Rev. William J. Prout of the Presbyterian Church read the scripture message; as the mortgage went up in flames, the congregation recited, *"We now burn this canceled mortgage, a symbol of a completed task, and dedicate ourselves anew to His service.*" The congregation was asked to remain standing as the mortgage was lighted and then join in singing the Doxology. It was noted at the service that the Dorcas class started the first building fund for the cornerstone of the new church at a meeting held at the home of Mrs. E. Hickson in the summer of 1917.

A balance was left in the Capital Funds after payment of the mortgage and open pledges yet to be received. These funds were being considered for redecoration and renovation of the church and the Sunday school building.

***

Children of the Sunday school had a birthday party at 2:30 in the afternoon in their classrooms with entertainment and motion pictures. This was how the year of the Sunday School Centennial (1850-1950) was celebrated.

The Founders of the Sabbath School women were dressed in period costumes.

L. to R.  Mabel Thomas, Polly Hunt, Regina Bevgner,
          Ella Thomas, Leone Titus, Angenette Ernisse.
Seated :  Mrs. Assnath Rogers

The following is the play that was presented on that day:

ONE HUNDRED YEARS AGO

Scene:  A farmhouse living room in Irondequoit
Time:   May 3, 1850
Characters:     Mrs. Adelaide Grant – Tarrant
                Mrs. Libbie Hagaman – Van Campen
                Mrs. Martha Woodworth – Smith

*(Adelaide Grant sits piecing a quilt, knitting, humming a hymn)*
A knock at the door:    Entrance of Martha and Libbie. They greet one another.

Libbie:     Oh, Addie, we've just finished our calling about the Sunday school and the library, and we want to talk over some of the plans for Sunday.

Adelaide:   Did you get enough money for some books?  Were people generous?

Martha:     Well, you know I told Libbie I would take her in my carriage if she would ask for the money – so we started out yesterday and went all the way to the toll gate and then over the Ridge and come down Garden Street and today...

Libbie:     *(Libbie interrupts)* And what do you think, Addie – we found only one man at home!  Imagine it! All those men down at the race track when they should be getting at the spring plowing.  It's a good thing the race only last three days out here or nobody would get their planting done on time!

Adelaide:   Then you didn't get anything?

Martha:     Oh yes, Libbie had good luck with the women anyway – everyone give something.  We collected nearly ten dollars yesterday and *(she dumps coins from a box)* I'll count what we got this morning.  *(She counts the money)*

Libbie:     We invited everyone to some Sunday afternoon to the schoolhouse.  And they promised to come or at least send the children.  I do hope there will be a good-sized group since Mr. Lee is coming and from Rochester.  He has organized so many Sunday Schools in the country; he'll know just how to get us started.

Adelaide:   I'm glad we could use the school.  There were getting to be too many children for home meetings – and with so many invited it will be nice to have a place big enough for all of us to meet together.

Martha:     Five dollars more – that's fifteen dollars altogether.  We ought to be able to get a start on the library with that.  Did I tell you that Mr. Lee's son, who is librarian at Brick Church, is going to help us choose the books?

Libbie:     When you go to the bookshop be sure to get a "minute book" to keep the attendance in.  I understand that if we get the Sunday school started, Mr. Lee will ask some of the Rochester pastors to come out and preach occasionally.

Adelaide:   It sounds almost too good to be true, doesn't it, that at last there will really be "Sunday" north of the Ridge!  Ever since Mr. Finney was in Rochester, it has seemed to me that we ought to do something out here.  Who is going to teach?

Libbie:     Mr. Lee said that some of the Brick church teachers will come out and help us if we need them.

Martha:     Well, to start with Chauncey and I are going to teach, and Libbie, of course, and we thought that maybe Sidney would...

Adelaide:   Yes, I think he will – and I think we should have Libbie take charge of the collections, too.  Harriet Blossom might be willing to take a class.  Later on we could ask Alfred Benedict or Henry Achille if enough people come.  Maybe Mr. Curtice would take charge of the library if we asked him.

Martha:     I have the key to the schoolhouse and since I'm right next door, I'll go over early so that no one will need to wait to get in.  Come on, Libbie, I'll drive you home – I have to get some baking done before Sunday.

Libbie:     Goodbye, Adelaide, we'll see you Sunday afternoon.  Just think – a Sunday school in Irondequoit at last!

        Curtain.

## The Church Reaches Out

In March of 1950, the Zaporoshzev family arrived in Rochester, New York. It was through the efforts of the members of the church under the leadership of the Rev. Lloyd R. Stamp, that the family was brought to this country.

Sponsored by the United Congregational Church of Irondequoit, the family, who had been staying in a refugee camp in the British zone of Austria, was chosen for emigration by the Church World Service. The family consisted of Peter, 18 and his father, Sergej, who had worked together as electricians on the street lights of Klagenfurt, where the camp was situated. The mother, Rosalia, worked in a British army mess hall, and the final member of the family, Sophia, was in charge of keeping the home in order as she was not old enough to get a work permit.

Sergej, a White Russian, escaped to Yugoslavia in 1920 after the Soviet revolution and in 1944 left Yugoslavia because of the Russians. While in Yugoslavia he met and married his wife, and both their children were born in Yugoslavia. The church furnished the family with an apartment, and once they were settled began the search for work. The church also helped them get into night school to take courses in English.

Mr. Zaporoshzev was quoted to have said, "Our hearts are so filled with gratitude to God for the blessing of being in this country and to have all the people of this church who have given us such a friendly and generous welcome that we long to overcome the barrier of language and express our thanks. We ask that they will continue to be understanding while we devote our very best efforts to the goal of becoming worthy citizens of this country."

The church's service to this family was well accepted and resulted in a successful conclusion. Mr. Zaporoshzev became a baker, his daughter Sophia, attended school and became a dancing instructor, while Peter entered the Air Force and was sent to Korea. Their success continued with Sergej's getting his U.S. citizenship.

Eighty Irondequoit residents gathered at the United Congregational Church for an anniversary dinner in honor of the Zaporoshzev family to show how proud they were of this family who had done such a splendid job of adjusting to their new lives in America.

Mr. and Mrs. Sergei Zaporoschzew and their children, Peter and Sonia

Changes were always on the horizon and most would become traditions. The presentation of a pageant, "The Nativity" under the direction of Mrs. Thorold Smith was a highlight of a church Christmas season which included a Sunday School Party, the lighting of the Church Christmas tree and the Christmas Eve candlelight Communion Service.

# The First Strawberry Festival

Another tradition would be the Strawberry Festival introduced in 1950. This was seen as a way to bring people into the church and by doing so hopefully increase the membership while putting on a fund raiser that everyone could enjoy.

The cost was 35 cents for the shortcake.

## The Story Of the "Sermon On The Mount" Painting

The United Congregational Church went a little bit Hollywood, they said, when they commissioned a Rochester artist, Batiste Madalena, of Genesee Park Boulevard, to create a painting. The church learned of Mr. Madalena through Mr. Redfern, who at the time worked as a window dresser for McCurdy's. Batiste at the time was the artist who painted the background for the window displays.

Madalena, who lived in Rochester all his life, first attracted attention as an original Hollywood movie poster creator, but he was a well-recognized portrait and mural artist. It was this skill that was sought by the church for a very specific reason.

At the end of the war, the Honor Roll committee began to study a suitable memorial for Robert Klippel and Raymond Pitts, who gave their lives in service. The committee felt that it should be a permanent memorial, in harmony with the simplicity of the church, and that its theme should be "peace." After considering many possible memorials, they decided to recommend a painting for the chancel[9]. The painting was approved at the annual meeting in early 1950 by a vote of 61 to 22. The work was completed by Madalena during the summer and the theme was "Christ on the Mount," selected with the feeling that the message of Jesus in the Sermon on the Mount is the most adequate foundation for a world of peace and brotherhood.

Batiste Madalena working on our *SERMON ON THE MOUNT* in his studio in Downtown Rochester

The painting was unveiled at a service of dedication held on October 15, 1950 by Mrs. C. H. Klippel and Mrs. S. Lloyd Redfern. Mr. William Clarke handled the presentation of the memorial painting, which was accepted by the Rev. Lloyd R. Stamp. A small bronze plaque was placed on the east wall of the vestibule of the church to identify the memorial painting. It bears a simple inscription: *"Dedicated to the memory of Robert Klippel and Raymond Pitts and in recognition of others from this church who served their country in World Wars I and II"* and is dated October 16, 1950.

---

[9] Area of the church near the altar

This painting is on the back wall of the sanctuary where everyone can see and enjoy it. With the addition of the painting, the World War II flag that had hung in the sanctuary throughout the war was taken down and put into storage.

Boy Scout Troop 154 was formed under the sponsorship of the Men's Club of the United Congregational Church of Irondequoit in February 1951. Mr. Sterling Torsleff was the first scoutmaster, Mr. Boris Worden the first troop committee chairman and Mr. Donald Keck the first senior patrol leader. There were nine scouts in the troop, which was presented its first charter in March of 1951.

## New York Congregational Christian Conference

By 1951 the troubled world was turning to the Christian church as a solid refuge. This was apparent when the Rev. Robert Bruce, minister and superintendent of the New York Congregational Christian Conference, opened the 118th Annual Meeting in the United Congregational Church of Irondequoit.  Rev. Bruce referred to church after church stating that they had seen their congregations double and even treble in the past years. Dr. Bruce declared this increase in church membership and attendance was attributable to the fact that the church is the only solid thing left to which one can cling.

The conference opened with a welcome by our pastor, the Rev. Floyd R. Stamp, which was followed by members of the staff of the New York office presenting their church involvement to the conference members.  A colorful procession of ministers in their clerical robes and scholastic hoods marked the evening worship and memorial service, which paid tribute to members of the clergy who had died since the previous annual meeting. The Rev. Edward L. Christie, minister of the First Congregational Church of Ithaca, delivered the conference sermon.

New York Congregational Christian Conference
Held In Irondequoit NY

## Increasing The Sunday School Building

By 1950 the church determined the need to increase the size of the Sunday school building as the number of children was growing with the community. In May 1951 the services of a professional architect were retained, and preliminary plans were provided for review. The plans were in harmony with the present structure, calling for extensive remodeling and rearrangement, plus a two-story structure added to the rear of the existing Sunday school building. They needed to consider controlled heating, adequate quarters for Boy and Girl Scouts, youth groups and adult organizations.

## Building Fund Raisers Begin Again

In April 1952 bids were received from four general contractors and several subsidiary contractors for the work called for by the Sunday school expansion plans. The bids were higher than expected, so no action was taken. Instead the church began presenting ways to raise the money needed.

On Wednesday, February 20, 1952, a concert was offered with sacred music, folk tunes and Negro spirituals to benefit the church building fund. Miss Wedow was the soprano soloist and Richard Clark the boy soprano, along with the 25-voice choir led by Mrs. Margaret Maxwell.

Another opportunity presented itself in the form of the 100th birthday of Mrs. Asenath Rogers on May 31, 1952, when they got the idea to invite one hundred of her friends to contribute a dollar in her honor to the Sunday school building fund.

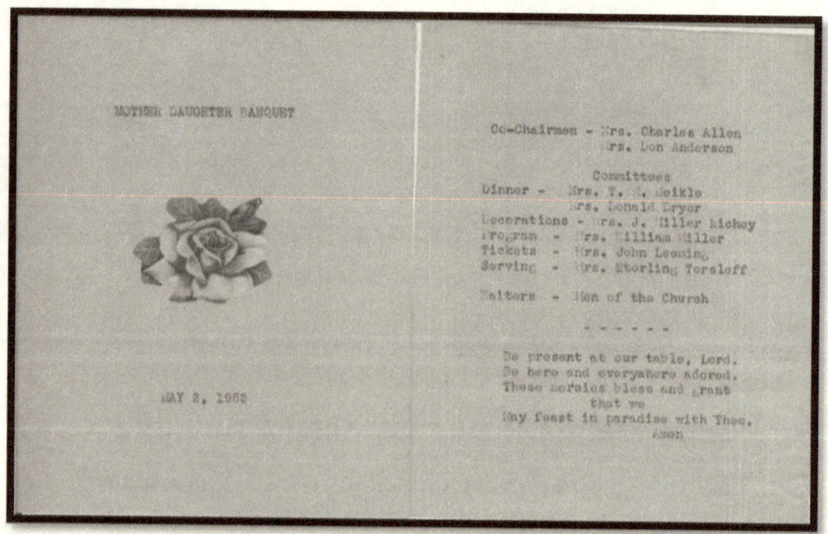


In May 1952, a mother-daughter banquet was held presenting the history of bridal gowns. The presentation was open to the general public with an announcement in the newspaper and the designing of the attractive program that appears above.

The sale of individual bricks for the new Sunday school addition was a project undertaken by the minister's children. Dorothy and David Stamp, who placed money in a bank to save toward the purchase of bricks for the new addition. The following announcement was printed to support their fund raising effort.

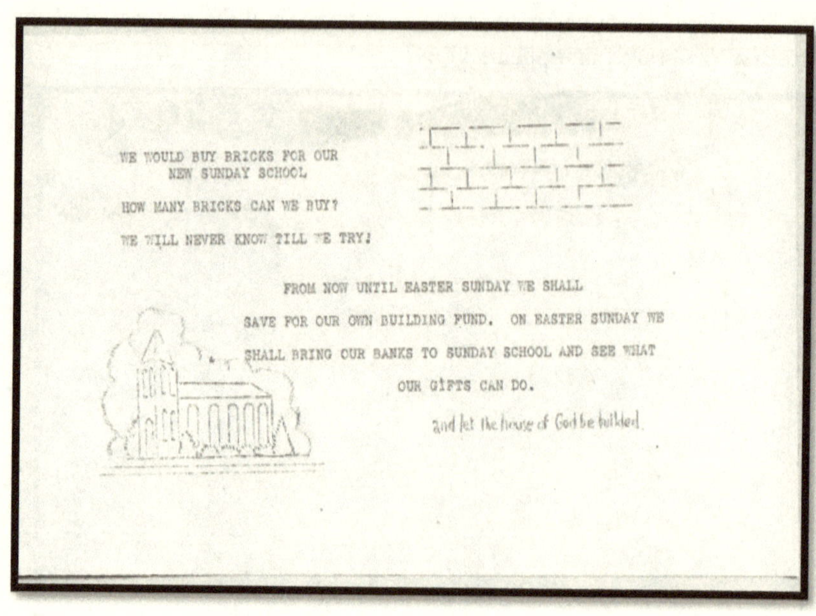


At the same time an important court decision was handed down by the Appellate Division of the New York Court dealing with the proposed merger of the Congregational Christian and Evangelical and Reformed Churches. This four-to-one decision on April 14, 1952 reversed the previous decision of January 26, 1950, which blocked the plans for the merger. The decision stated that "civil courts do not interfere with ecclesiastical matters of churches in which temporal rights are not involved."

**Charles Harrison, Rev., Lloyd Stamp, Bill Klein & Thorold Smith at 1952 Cornerstone Ceremony**

As the 104th year of Sunday school history became a connecting link between the inspiring past and the challenging future, "things new" seemed to be its keynote because 1953 brought the Sunday school a new building, new facilities and equipment, new classes and departments, new ways to meet new needs, new records of enrollment and attendance, new staff members, new interpretations of old patterns and, as always, new opportunities.

**Putting Packet In the 1952 Corner Stone**

The United Congregational Cornerstone Rites were held in 1952. The brief program included the depositing of mementos in a copper box placed inside the cornerstone. Participating in the program were the Rev. Lloyd R. Stamp, Minister, Thorold G. Smith, Vice Chairman, and The Board Of Trustees.

## Traditions Are Built Upon

In 1953, a tradition that had begun in 1950 continued as the third annual Strawberry Festival, sponsored jointly by the Men's Club and the Women's Guild of the United Congregational Church, was held on a Friday in June. The grounds behind the church were arranged with tables and chairs to accommodate the ever-increasing throng attending this now well-attended affair. The old-fashioned festival featured strawberries served with ice cream or plain strawberries with home-made shortcake. Each choice came with a topping of homemade whipped cream. By now it was becoming also a tradition for any upcoming community or church event to be widely publicized and this lead to an ever growing attendance.

***

It was a sad day when the news arrived that on August 9, 1954, Mr. Zaporoshzev passed away. The Zaporoshzev family who had been sponsored b the church to come to America, had remained faithful members of the church family.  His passing was deeply felt by each and every church member as the family were involved members in the church.

***

The creation in the fall of 1953 of a new lower-junior department for third- and fourth-grade classes was blessed with an enrollment of over one hundred. Around the same time they established an Adult Fellowship Group and an all-inclusive adult Sunday school class that met under the pastor's leadership. The groups met weekly for religious discussion and monthly for a special programs. These program additions were also well received and attended.

With Mrs. Thorold G. Smith as supervisor, a teacher training class for high school girls was started, which was looked upon as an eventual source of experienced leaders and even today contributes valuable service in the primary church program.

The provision of leadership for the children's extended period required some rethinking. Through the Board of Christian Education, experimental steps were taken during 1953 to put this phase of service on a new and more satisfactory basis.  The kindergarten department used a monthly teacher-rotation system, the primary department received the aid of the new teacher training class, and the lower-junior department hoped eventually to secure parental cooperation to assist Mrs. Charles Plomasen in helping out during church activities.

The formation of a house committee to supervise scheduling and other arrangements for the use of building facilities and a rules committee to be responsible for sponsorship, chaperoning and time and space regulations were also new solutions to new problems arising from the enlarged quarters and the expanded program.


## Rev. Walter A. Telfer (1955-1963)

At the end of 1954, the Rev. Lloyd Stamp resigned to accept a call as pastor in a new church to be organized in Levittown, PA. Rev.

Walter A. Telfer. Since his installation, the congregation had reached 975 members. So many accomplishments had occurred during his leadership and though sorry to see him go, the congregation was happy for his new opportunity.

Walter A. & Mrs. Tefler

It was also a time when the Memorial Fund for the church was continuing to grow through the generosity of members and friends. Seventy-nine memorial gifts totaled nearly $800.00, and the pledges for the year were around $17,150.

In 1955, the Board of Trustees entered negotiations for the sale of the parsonage located on Hudson Avenue. This sale was to be handled in conjunction with the building of the new parsonage. The parsonage sold for around $12,000, providing sufficient funding for the new parsonage.

The New Church Parsonage On Hudson Avenue

## Finishing The New Church Addition

The growth of the Sunday school led to the successful finishing of its first year of operation under the double-session plan in 1956. Because of the size of the congregation, it was decided to hold two services each Sunday and the change was well accepted. During 1957, 102 memorial gifts were made, and the income level grew to a little over $1,600.00

With the contractor's completion of the essential framework of the new Sunday school building in March of 1957, a church-wide volunteer work project to finish and decorate the interior began, and as the six-month program progressed, 140 persons gave more than 3000 hours of service and achieved varying degrees of expertise in such unfamiliar tasks as painting, tile laying, sealing, sound-proofing, cleaning and varnishing. In the course of these activity, carried on as work nights and work days sponsored by various groups and organizations, more than a ton of wall sealer was applied in preliminary coating; nearly sixty gallons of paint transformed drab walls to cheerful yellows, browns, greens, blues and grays; eight thousand floor tiles were laid (some in the old building as well as in the new area); and four thousand tiles were set in ceilings.

Although it is impossible to name all who gave so generously of their energies and their time, recognition must be given to Mr. and Mrs. Charles Allen for their tireless organization and patient supervision of work units; to Russell Rankin, Donald Dryer and Carl Amrine for countless hours of toil; and to the two ministers, Rev. Stamp and Rev. Billups, who contributed their time and labor beyond the call of duty.

The cooperation and generosity of many groups and individuals who provided labor made the added space usable by Rally Day time. Rally Day, Christian Education Sunday, Kick-Off Sunday, Sunday School Round-Up; are all names assigned to getting the education program going in the fall. Rally Day was a strong recruitment tool by the 1910s. Rally Day is observed in some congregations to celebrate a new start or a renewed effort in involving children, youth, and adults in Sunday morning classes for Christian education. When Rally Day is observed on its own, focus is on efforts to involve as much of the congregation as possible in Sunday school or other Christian formation opportunities.

The Women's Guild assumed a large share of responsibility, curtaining the new windows, equipping the youth center kitchenette and furnishing the cradle room, and Circle gifts provided hymnals, book shelves, chairs, tables and other needed items in many departments. Special designations had been made from the Memorial Fund for worship centers in two assembly rooms.

The Sunday school was grateful to Mr. and Mrs. Elmer Lalonde for the gift of a film strip and slide projector, which proved invaluable in the expanded visual aid program.

## Enrollment & Attendance Grows

A study of the recording secretary's annual report during the period of 1953-1956 showed new gains in enrollment and in attendance, both in individual Sunday totals and in overall averages. The largest attendance in the prior twelve years was a record on Children's Day, June 14, when 700 attended the combined church and

Sunday school service. The presentation of over one hundred Bibles to graduating primary pupils on Promotion Sunday in June also set another new record.

With a peak registration of 126 boys and girls representing twenty different churches of ten denominations, the Vacation Church School, directed by the Rev. Joseph C. Billups for two weeks in July, set a few records of its own. A staff of sixteen assisted Rev. Billups in carrying out this annual program. The figures placed the United Congregational among the five largest Sunday schools in the Rochester area. The growth in enrollment continued, leading to the formation of new classes and the need for more teachers to join the staff of veterans who loyally served the Sunday school year after year.

In 1958 a monthly tradition of the Hymn of the Month began. This tradition was the choosing of a less familiar hymn each month; the history of that hymn appeared in the church newsletter. Each Sunday during that month, the hymn was sung so that the congregation might come to know some of the great but lesser-known hymns of the church.

It was midyear of 1958 when the Rev. Margaret Frerichs, the minister of religious education, resigned after accepting a call to be a pastor of the Congregational Church of Lyme, New Hampshire. The search for a replacement began immediately, and by September of that year Miss Elizabeth Hyde was the new Minister of Religious Education. Unfortunately the weekly religious education was discontinued by the churches of West Irondequoit because of parents' and students' lack of interest.

***

The church had grown not only in membership but in the size and shape of the church itself as the new additions were added to keep up with the growing congregation. Yet, through all of the structural and family changes, the church continued to be a United church.

Finally, homecoming weekend was held in May of 1961 nearest the date of the founding of the Sunday school on May 5,1850. This occasion was celebrated with a pageant covering the history of the Sunday School.

***

During that year's summer months, the church was also involved in a new venture, inviting twenty-nine youngsters from an inner city church—Corn Hill Methodist Church—to join twenty-four Irondequoit youngsters at the church's annual weeklong vacation school. Each morning, five United Church mothers picked up the inner city children and brought them to the 2 ½-hour sessions they called "Unlocking Secrets." They offered group projects along with singing, stories, lessons, recreation and refreshments. There was also a short worship service at the end of each session. In total there were nine women teachers and ten teenage aides in charge of the vacation school, which proved successful.

116

# The Fifty Year Golden Celebration

Around this same time a committee was formed to begin the preparations for the fiftieth anniversary of the United Congregational Church[10]. The committee chairman was Mr. Thorne. At this meeting they decided on four events, starting in the fall of 1960 and continuing through the spring of 1961. The first event was held in October or November of 1960 on the weekend nearest the exact date of the laying of the marker for the WCTU Building, and the celebration centered around a skit about the WCTU. Then in January 1961, the Annual Meeting of the church honored charter members with a display of pictures and records.  This event was followed by a rededication of the church in March 1961, on the Sunday nearest the fiftieth anniversary of the receipt of the charter of the church. Mrs. Rudman Sherman presented a talk on the church history, and she prefaced her history as she had done for the first twenty-five years with an anonymous verse.

*Tonight the golden bells ring out*
*The chimes sound bright and clear*
*As once again we celebrate*
*An Anniversary Year.*

On October 25, 1961 the church marked its fiftieth anniversary. In keeping with the candle-service tradition, the Sunday school candle was lit by Margaret Anderson Willis, the granddaughter of George H. Rudman. The WCTU candle was lit by Betty Dake Holland, granddaughter of Celia Dake, long-time president of the WCTU. Smaller candles represented a decade of church life. Grace Slater, a charter member, celebrated the fiftieth anniversary with a candle-lighting service in honor and remembrance of the church founders.

---

[10] The United Church of Christ came into being in 1957, but the name had yet to be changed.

**Candle Lighting Ceremony at the 50th Anniversary**

The candle service included the following presentation:

*The United Church really began not 50 but 111 years ago—in 1850—when Irondequoit Union Sabbath School was founded. Because our church was first created in the hearts of devoted laymen and women who wanted more Christian teaching for the children of Irondequoit, we first light the Sunday school candle.*
**(Margaret Anderson Willis lit this candle.)**
*Thirty years later some of the women of the Sunday school, with others in the town, established the Irondequoit Chapter of the WCTU. Through the efforts of this group, a meeting place was provided for the Sunday school, and through its generosity the church came into possession of its first home. So the*

*WCTU candle received its light from that of the
Sunday school.*
**(Betty Dake Holland lit the WCTU candle.)**
*The zeal of these two organizations kept the spark
of desire for local church services glowing until,
in 1911, it culminated in the establishment of the
United Congregational Church. Both candles are
needed to light the Church candle.*
**(Mrs. Willis and Mrs. Holland lit the Church
candle.)**
*The 1911 candle represents the first years of our
church life and all the first things that reflect the
thrilling beginning of a great venture of faith. In
gratitude, we light this candle for our early years.*
**(Mr. Clarke/Mr. Warren lit this Church candle.)**
*The next decade was a time of inspiration and
building, during which this beautiful house of
worship came into being. With thankful hearts we
light the second candle, for the years between
1921 and 1931.*
**(Mr. DeSmit/Mrs. Bristol lit the 1911 candle.)**
*Then followed a period of trial and tribulation,
during which faith was tested and sacrifice
demanded. Somehow hope endured. The candle
of the 1931 decade is one of love and
commitment. Its shining light honors those of our
number who went that difficult second mile.*
**(Mrs. Dye and Mrs. Groth lit the 1931 candle.)**
*Renewal was the keynote of the next ten years.
Strength returned to lighten the burden of debt.
Vigor and enthusiasm met the challenge of new
tasks. The spirit of earlier times was rekindled in
the 40s.*
**(Mr. Dryer lit the 1941 candle.)**
*Growth in numbers, enlargement of opportunities
to serve, expansion of facilities—these
characterize our church in the decade just
ending. As we light the candle of progress, we*

*pray that its flame may reveal spiritual
development as well.*
**(Mrs. Mackey lit this candle.)**
*This is our candle of hope for the future, lighted
in 1961 in remembrance and rededication, with
the hope that the years of the past may ever
inspire the years to come, to carry their light to
the ends of the earth.*
**(Robert Wiegand lit the 1961 candle.)**

The service concluded with the poem **"God's Candles We"** that was used in the 25th anniversary service and with the prayer used at that time. The congregation joined in singing three verses of **"O Light from Age to Age the Same."**

For the 50th Anniversary ceremony, Mrs. Benjamin Titus, an early member of the WCTU, prepared a short history of the Irondequoit WCTU that included some little-known details, such as that the contract for the building was left to Joseph Smart and that the Hall was dedicated on June 14, 1885. The building and site cost $1946.00, but not until 1887 was the property free from indebtedness. Sheds for horses were subsequently built at a cost of $300. With the future additions to the building the total cost came to $4800.

The United Congregational Church began a yearlong celebration for the church's golden anniversary. The celebration included the marker rededication. The marker had been temporarily removed in reconstruction of an entrance to the church building; Mrs. Rogers had designated the fund use to the resetting project before her death in 1957.

Twenty four of the thirty-six surviving charter members were in attendance, along with Howard Tyler, grandson of Mrs. Rogers, and three of the original members: Mrs. George West, Vice President of the former WCTU Chapter; Miss Leone Titus, daughter of Mrs. Benjamin Titus, WCTU President for sixteen years; and Frank Grant, grandson of Mrs. Sidney B. Grant, WCTU member and a founder of the Sunday school sixty-one years before the church was organized.

    The Rev. Walter Telfer presided over the ceremonies with the assistance of the Rev. Leslie Strathern and John Thorne, Chairman of the 50th-Anniversary Committee.

**The Dinner At The 50th Celebration**

Letters went out and responses were received to attend the celebration, and former ministers were invited. Two of those responses are shown here.

Whitman, Mass.
July 20, 1960

Dear People of the Irondequoit Church:

Thank you for the reminder. It is indeed getting late and the time of your Fiftieth Anniversary Celebration is near at hand.

It seems impossible that it is nearly fifty years since I became your pastor. I wish to congratulate you on living and working together for this half-century. I hope that you will continue, and in another fifty years will again celebrate.

I remember the first services of United Church in which I participated. Over 200 charter members were taken into the church, I believe. I had never baptized so many at one time. I have many happy memories of my years with you.

I shall await with interest a notice of our program, and a copy of any booklet you choose to prepare. My daughter, Barbara, who acts as my secretary, will type this for me.

With love and greetings to you all,
Harold S. Capron

---

Staunton, Va.
June 24, 1960

A message of greeting:
To all of my friends in a dearly beloved church.

The development of United Church through all these years is a marvelous accomplishment that has brought the fulfillment of a very much needed and longed for end.

I will not attempt to mention the names of those who had the most to do with this consummation of faith and hope. I have never known or ever heard of people so devoted and generous in all respects. I know that if it were possible for me to be there, and it isn't there would be a great number of dear familiar faces I would miss.

If I could , nothing would have pleased me better than to send you a message of spiritual congratulations I have one txt in mind and that is "Speak unto the children of Israel that they go forward." This I know you will do.

With my earnest prayers for all your plans, that they may be fulfilled to your complete joy and peace, and with my profoundest affection, I am
Sincerely,
William J. Prout

As part of the service, the children in the church school presented an interpretation of seven continuing facets of Christian worship: Christ, the Bible, the hymnal, the cross, the Christian flag, the offering plate and the cup.  This presentation was followed by a supper.

The next celebration of the evening was slides that depicted events in the history of the church. The slides were reproduced from old photographs prepared by Samuel Vaisey. The Rev. Leslie Strathern, associate minister, prepared the script for the slides.

Previous Sunday school members recalled events of a half century prior with the first of four special programs. The celebration program extended through the following June. At the close of the Sunday service, the church dedicated the resetting of the WCTU marker in the front wall of the old church building. The marker, a cement tablet, commemorated the gift of the building to the church by the WCTU. The tablet was first installed high on the building above the front doors to the Sunday school. When the building was altered somewhat in 1925 to blend in with the new church sanctuary that was built adjacent to it, the marker was reset in a wall forming the base of stairs to the front doors. The stairs were subsequently changed and the marker removed and stored in the basement.

The late Mrs. Hosea Rogers, an influential member of the WCTU and the Sunday school, subsequently designated a financial gift for the resetting of the marker. It was her wish that the close ties between the WCTU, the Sunday school and the church not be forgotten. The Irondequoit WCTU unit ceased operation in the early 1940s. At the time of the fiftieth anniversary, the church membership was around 1,400 and the minister was Rev. Walter A. Telfer, who served as the pastor for the Irondequoit Congregational Church from 1955 until 1963.

**Reception Line At The 50th Celebration**

The final event in the 50th anniversary celebration was the homecoming weekend program. The congregational church had more than 4400 members at some point and nearly 1500 names were on the membership roll by the end of 50 years .

When the Soviet Union launched Sputnik 1 in October of 1957, the bond of gravity that tied man to the planet earth was broken, and space was suddenly open to exploration.  Within a few years visits to the moon by U. S. astronauts became almost commonplace and unmanned space vehicles sent back valuable scientific information from other planets.

This space age technology came at a time when the earth inhabitants seemed driven to destroy one another and possibly themselves.  Two nuclear superpowers, the United States and the Soviet Union were locked in a cold war and destruction became a very real possibility during the crises over Berlin and Cuba.

The mood of the space age was largely one of protest and increasing violence as greater gulfs opened between black and white, young and old, rich and poor.  Many countries saw the decline of the growth earlier in economics as the decade drew to a close.  This was a time when the earth saw the threats of overpopulation, pollution of the air and water, and the exhaustion of numerous natural resources.

In 1963, the Central Committee of the World Council of Churches assembled at the University of Rochester and then met at Colgate Rochester Divinity School in a truly international convocation that included Soviet Russia. Virginia Mackey, John Thorne and Eleanor Miller acted as officials, and twenty-five of the young adults served as stewards, runners and technicians. It seemed fitting, after acting as host in 1960 for the New York State Conference of the Congregational Church, that in 1963 the church should now join with Salem

Evangelical and Reformed Church in hosting the New York State Conference of the United Congregational Church, which established our present affiliations and title.

Around this time, the church was again saying goodbye to their pastor.

There was a thirteen-month span before the search committee found their new pastor, Dr. Wilbour Eddy Saunders, past President of Colgate Rochester Divinity School, who after befriending and serving us in many crucial ways for years, not only acted as Interim Pastor but served on church councils and boards.

***

There was a bid in the black community to bring Florence Alinsky, a prominent civil rights leader and advocate of black power, to Rochester and at the time it was met with fierce opposition by many. In the midst of the controversy Alinsky sent two of his associates, Ed

Chambers and Ron Jones, to the Flower City to begin to organize the Black community. Florence was chosen to head the steering committee of the newly formed community based black activist organization that was given the name FIGHT; an acronym for Freedom, Integration, God, Honor, Today (the "I" was changed in 1967 to stand for "Independence"). For Alinsky, it was paramount that communities organize themselves. He remained in the background in the role of consultant and white liberals interested in the civil rights movement in Rochester were asked to step aside and allow blacks to speak for themselves. These white activists formed Friends of FIGHT (later to become Metro Act) which developed alongside FIGHT as a separate organization. Florence was formally elected president of FIGHT at the first annual FIGHT convention in June 1965. He held the presidency from 1965-1967 and again in 1968.

Rochester's urban problems were typical of many northern cities which experienced a rapid immigration of blacks from the south between 1950 and 1970. As white residents and businesses moved to the suburbs, inner city blacks faced high unemployment, poor housing and substandard schools. FIGHT's mission was to address this defacto segregation and the social problems that resulted from it. FIGHT pledged to train unskilled blacks and move them into the prosperous Rochester economy, to develop and renew urban neighborhoods, to create quality education and, perhaps most importantly, to develop political activism and community participation amongst poor urban blacks.

Dr. Saunders was active in the Rochester Council of Churches' transition over FIGHT. (Several years later, after serving as right-hand man to the Rev. Robert Bermudes in his early years here, he was Rev. Bermudes' chief mentor during his doctorial studies.) He was an inspiring figure and continued to serve in any way he could until his death in 1979.

***

It seemed that the need for a church grew as the United States entered one war after another. By far the longest military conflict in U.S. history was the Vietnam War, from 1959 to April 30, 1975. The hostilities in Vietnam, Laos, and Cambodia claimed the lives of more than 58,000 Americans. Another 304,000 were wounded.

The congregation provided aid and assistance where it was needed while the church moved forward.

## Action Moviemaking Group (Later VISCOM)

It was during this period that the formation of the Action Moviemaking group took place. The main point of the moviemaking group was to lead kids to Christ through Love first and second, to help them to grow up to be good citizens before man and God.  It also provided a unique understanding of Movie Making Basics which included a discussion on the needs of the group:

Producer: The person who arranges the finances and hires the actors

Director: A person who supervises the creative aspects of a movie and instructs the actors on-stage.

Gaffer: An electrician who deals with lighting.

Grip: A stagehand who helps adjust sets and props and sometimes assist the cameraman.

Foley Artist: A sound effects person.

Story Boards: A set of drawings that show every camera angle for every shot. A typical movie would have thousands of story boards. They are used to help explain each shot to each person involved in making the project.

Script or shot sheet: Lays out each shot in order with the text on the left side of the page and a description of the camera position on the right. A line is drawn across the page under each shot.

This group went on to present movies, slides and provide the technical assistance needed for the church.

* * *

Bob Hawks, a church member in the marines in Vietnam, wrote a letter speaking of the shortage of military necessities such as helmets and guns. He also told of the disease, the danger of sunstroke, the leeches and the viciousness of the enemy.  While the war raged on, violence of another type was brewing at home.

Race riots added to the conflict and unrest. Rochester's racial disturbances in 1964 and their aftermath were characterized by violence and looting; in a period of approximately sixty hours, there were four deaths, at least 350 injuries, over 800 arrests, and property damage totaling more than a million dollars. The riot was precipitated by the arrest of an allegedly drunk and disorderly African-American man at a Joseph Avenue street dance. But even in its immediate aftermath, many looked to underlying social and environmental conditions to explain the events that followed. The National Guard was called in to keep the peace. Rochester was dubbed "Smugtown" in the 1950s because of the comfort and complacency borne of its economic prosperity and amicable labor-management relations fostered by the Eastman Kodak Company and other large, successful, high-tech corporations.

The riots represented a profound blow to Rochester's positive self-image. As the flames of discontent were replaced by the glare of the media spotlight, black and white Rochester residents were forced to reflect, from different perspectives and with different conclusions, on the causes and meanings of this devastating event.

# Rev. Harleigh M. Rosenberger (1965-1972)

Harleigh M. & Mrs. Rosenberger

After serving as the Interim Reverend, Rev. Saunders stepped aside in 1965 when Harleigh Rosenberger accepted the post as the new minister for the United Church.  A series of small "get-acquainted" gatherings were held among the 1,500 members of the IUCC to help the Rosenberger's meet the congregation.  The Rosenbergers would live in the current church parsonage at 56 Ganado Road, while the Associate minister, Rev. Donald M. Wilson resided at a second parsonage at 2631 Oakview Drive.

The Rev. Rosenberger said, "Let us honestly seek ways to be of positive help in these tremendous problems of human relationships, not stumbling blocks over which others must jump in order to create progress."  These were the right words at the right time. The Rev. Rosenberger, raised a Mennonite and ordained a Baptist, served the United Congregational Church in Irondequoit from 1965 until 1972. His installation appropriately coincided with the beginning of the worldwide observance of the Week of Prayer for Christian Unity.

Although he could have served the United Congregational Church while remaining a Baptist, he decided to join the Congregational faith. With his foresightedness and pleasing disposition, the church did well.

## The Need For A New Organ

In 1966 an organ committee was formed to investigate the possibility of repairing the pipe organ. The committee invited seven organ builders to give estimates. Every one stated the church's money would be better spent on a new instrument than pouring more money into an old organ built by a firm then out of existence.

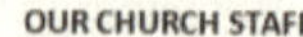

Left to right - Mrs. Geraldine Neubauer, Secretary to Associate Minister and Director of Christian Education; Mrs. Joyce Caravetta, Organist and Choir Director; Mrs. Gertrude Bennion, Church Secretary: the Reverend Donald M. Wilson, Associate Minister; The Reverent Harleigh M. Rosenberger, Senior Minister; Mr. Thomas Reardon, Assistant Custodian.
Not in Picture - The Reverend Simon Haynes, Custodian; Mr. & Mrs. William Tasker, Custodians.

When Pastor Rosenberger presented the findings to the congregation, he began by priding the history of their current seventy-year-old organ built in 1926. He enlightened the congregation on the issue of the reputable firm of Hook and Hastings of Boston, which had built the wonderful organ but which, after 100 years of service, had been forced out of business during the depression. Pastor Rosenberger expressed the need to consider purchasing a new organ, since the needed parts were then impossible to obtain.

The figures presented to the pastor by the committee were $2,000 for the cost for repair of the pipes and later $4,000 to $5,000 for releathering[11]. They advised that the church consider purchasing a new organ, which was estimated to cost $40,000 but would eliminate the need for any repairs in the near future.

Because of the interest in helping to defray the cost, an organ memorial fund was created in honor of Joyce Caravetta, the then-church organist who designed a superb replacement for the old organ.

---

[11] There is a small piece of leather associated with every pipe of the organ. That's 3,245 pipes. This piece of leather is a thin round disk between 3-to-4 inches in diameter. It varies in size according to the size of pipe it controls. It's about the size of a coaster you place under a glass so as not to mar a table.

With the design and the acumen of the committee that was headed by Thomas Meikle and Jack Debenham, enough organ bonds were sold to the members of the church.  The organ, insured for $125,000, was dedicated and installed in 1969.

Made by Keates Organ Company of Acton, Ontario, the organ had thirty-eight ranks of pipes and cost $50,000; this would be a one-of-a-kind organ, as selected parts of the old organ were included with the new. With its combination of delicacy and power, this organ became a sought-after instrument for recitals.  Although the installation was to be completed by February 15, it was not completed until June, with its full capabilities yet to be explored through the performance of works by Purcell, Swelinck, J. S. Bach, Reger, Couperin, Mozart and Hindemith.

The year was proving to be one of change. On January 16, 1964 the Constitution and By-Laws for the Church was presented and adopted.

By 1965 the church had a membership of over 1500, making the responsibilities of the staff quite complex. A list was prepared to show the primary responsibilities of each staff member.

A notable accomplishment in 1965 was the First Ecumenical Service of Catholics and Protestants. Catholics and Protestants prayed and sang together at one of the nation's first ecumenical services. The historic service was held at the Congregational Church of Irondequoit, where priests and ministers alike led prayers, a Presbyterian choir sang and a Jesuit preached the sermon.

Sponsored by six Protestant and three Catholic churches of West Irondequoit, the service marked the first local implementation of the decree on ecumenism of the Second Vatican Council. It called on Catholics not only to engage in dialogue and in other common witness with other churches, but also to pray for the cause of Christian unity. The business suit typical of reformed Protestant clergy and flowing black robes and magenta capes mingled in the opening procession. .

In 1965, the church began sponsorship of Chan Yee Ling in the amount of $60 every six months. This sponsorship continued until June of 1969.

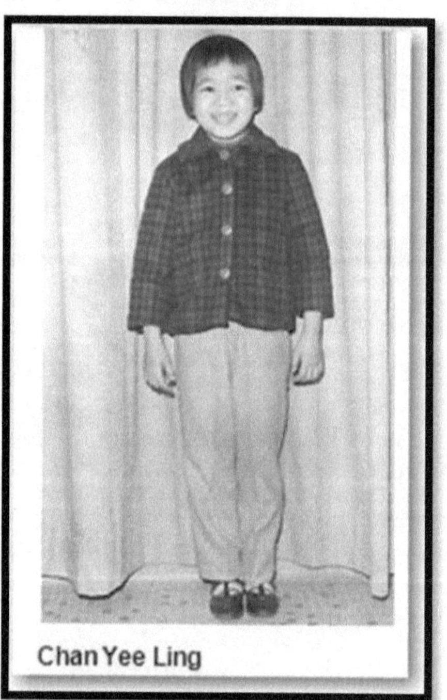

Chan Yee Ling

In 1967 the church instituted a weekly newsletter, "The Lighted Cross," a most important innovation, taking from the past designs, contents and need to know layouts.

Because of the size of the memorial fund that continued to grow, it was around this time that the Memorial Committee was formed and immediately began its service.

Not only did the committee oversee the fund

account, they were constantly
looking for areas of
involvement.

## The Memorial Garden

In between the
buildings of the United
Church was a space, viewed
from the walkway to the
Sanctuary.  The Memorial
Committee decided to plant
and other wise enhance this
area.  The space became
known as The Memorial
Garden..

The memorial
garden, though small had a
great impact on the building
beautification and would be
expanded on further in the
future.

## Dedication Service For The New Organ

In October of 1969, a dedicatory recital of the new organ was
held at the church. The recital was presented by Mrs. Paul D. Caravetta.
On the Sunday before Christmas, the Senior Choir sang "The
Christmas Story" by Heinrich Schutz.  Heinrich Schultz is credited with
being the first to set the complete biblical story of the birth of Christ to
music back in 1664 and as such has been described as the first German
Oratorio.  Soloists for the work included J. Miller Richey, Arthur
Hulse, and Gerald Bushart, tenors; Jeannine Lawrence, soprano; John
VanCampen, Eugene MacConnell, Sylvester Partridge and Richard
Aust, basses; Betty Fyles, Charlotte Lewis and Lauretta Richey, altos.

The Music Director of the church, Joyce Caravetta, provided organ
accompaniment and directed the performance.

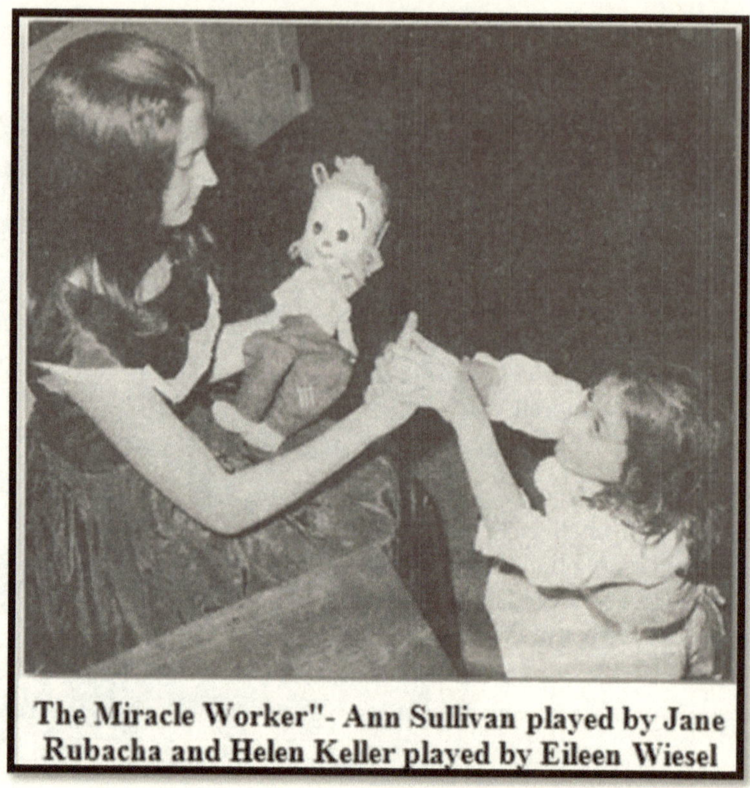

The Miracle Worker"- Ann Sullivan played by Jane
Rubacha and Helen Keller played by Eileen Wiesel

Keeping with their tradition of artistic ability, in 1970 the
Action Drama group of the Senior High Fellowship presented the play
*The Miracle Worker*," by William Gibson, the story of Annie Sullivan,
the first teacher of Helen Keller. In preparation for this play, the youth
group toured the Rochester School for the Deaf and learned sign
language so the play would be as authentic as possible. The
presentation was dedicated in memory of Mrs. Donald Dryer, a former
member of the church.

## Becoming the Irondequoit United Church Of Christ

The United Church of Christ (UCC) , a mainline Protestant Christian denomination principally in the United States, was formed in 1957 with the union of the Evangelical and Reformed Church and the Congregational Christian Churches. These churches in turn arose from the merger of earlier Protestant churches in the United States, through which the denomination traces its roots back to the Protestant Reformation.

The UCC has full communion with several other Protestant denominations and participates in worldwide ecumenical efforts. With favored progressive or liberal views on civil rights, gay rights, women's rights, abortion, and other social issues, the church fit into the mold of what the congregation wished to become. The open minded outlook as well as the United Church of Christ congregations having freedom in matters of doctrine and ministry, proved interesting.

The UCC uses four words to describe itself: "Christian, Reformed, Congregational and Evangelical." The church's diversity and adherence to covenantal polity (rather than government by regional elders or bishops) give individual congregations a great deal of freedom in the areas of worship, congregational life, and doctrine.

The motto of the United Church of Christ "That they may all be one," was impressive

Irondequoit had no church buildings before 1911, when the United

Congregational Church, was erected.  The origin of this church was in a Sunday School established in 1850 with the Sunday School services held in the nearby school-house until, in 1884, the W. C.T. U. Hall was built. Here, evening church services were conducted by students from the Rochester Theological Seminary. When this hall was destroyed by fire on October 29, 1909, a new building was immediately constructed to take its place but, before completed, it was decided to organize a church. The comment of those days that "There's no religion north of the Ridge" was hardly fair, since interested town's people were at that time attending various city churches. The new building was dedicated on January 22, 1911 and the Reverend Harold Capron of the South Congregational Church of Rochester was called as its first pastor.

The cornerstone of the new Congregational Church was laid on May 30, 1926 and the building dedicated on February 27, 1927. At that time, the original building became the Sunday School, to which an addition was constructed in 1952.  All of these facts were taken into consideration before changing the name of the church.

In the end, The Irondequoit Congregational Church welcomed the change to the Irondequoit United Church of Christ with the complete control of their finances, hiring and firing of clergy and other staff, and theological and political stands.

An outstanding accomplishment in 1970 was the Community Service Award presented to the Senior High Action Youth Fellowship of Irondequoit United Church of Christ. This award was presented by Parent's Magazine for outstanding service to the community during 1969-70. The youth earned the award by serving as teachers and aides at Rochester Eastside Community House, helping a needy inner-city family, assisting the Red Cross Bloodmobile and redecorating the Association for the Blind Headquarters.

The teen group was divided into nine action groups for service and personal enrichment. The newest of the nine action groups was the Action Travel Seminar. Members of this group raised funds for an exchange program with church young people and church families in Europe. The Acton Outreach group called on every member of the church to deliver the brotherhood symbol and a printed explanatory sheet, with the request that the symbol be displayed in their front window. They also made available to the business community of Irondequoit an up-to-date listing of phosphate levels on brand-name detergents and contributed $50 to the Walk for Water. The Action Drama presented three plays: "The Leader," "Not Enough Rope" and If Men Played Cards as Women Do." The Action Christian Education was involved in the church school as teaching assistants. Action Inreach organized a room in the church building as a meeting place for senior highs. Their Action Stage Band provided entertainment for hospitals and nursing homes and in the church coffeehouse, and the Action Movie Making Group engaged in shedding light on current social issues through film.

In January of 1971, a combined ecumenical prayer service was sponsored by the West Irondequoit Ministerial Association and held at St. Thomas the Apostle Roman Catholic Church with a film entitled "A Life in the Day of a Boy," produced by the Irondequoit United Church of Christ Youth Fellowship. There was also a fellowship drama group that interpreted the Lord's Prayer and a forty-voice choir from Summerville Presbyterian Church that sang "One World," by Bratten O'Hara and "Hallelujah Amen!" by Handel.  Four Protestant and three Roman Catholic clergymen took part in the service for unity and peace.

# Rev. Robert W. Bermudes (1972-1993)

Robert W. & Mrs. Bermudes

In 1972, Rev. Rosenberger would resign his post as pastor. After an eight-month search for the individual who could best carry on and enlarge the ministry of the church and deepen its spiritual commitment, the Search Committee was successful in bringing the Rev. Robert W. Bermudes to Irondequoit United Church of Christ.

The Search Committee visited many ministers in many cities and invited some to come to preach. Mr. Bermudes came with experience and dedication.  With him came his wife, Sally, and their sons Robert, Mark and Peter.

This was a trying time for the new leader because of the increasing complexity of the church's program and the multiple leadership problems brought on by the gradual tripling of the congregation and the realization that the buildings needed repair and improvement. Even the business-management resources required amplification.  Rev. Bermudes was ready for the challenge.

## The First Crop Walk

In 1975 the first CROP Walk in Irondequoit began. A CROP Walk is neighbors walking together to take a stand against hunger in our world. Together it raises awareness and funds for international relief and development, as well as local hunger-fighting.

Formed by Sally Bermudes and assisted by Roy Holmes, the CROP Walk started at the IUCC building with members of the Irondequoit Town Band playing in the side yard.

The Crop Walks were organized by the Inter-Faith Council for Social Service in partnership with Church World Service.  In 1963, a group of seven local people united their volunteer efforts to address the conditions of poverty in Chapel Hill and Carrboro. Thus the Inter-Faith Council was created, "to discover unmet needs and to respond through the coordinated efforts of volunteers.". In 1963 IFC formed the Inter-Church Council to continue work of the Committee of Church Women United. Church World Service works with IFC to eradicate hunger and poverty and to promote peace and justice around the world. They reach out to neighbors in need near and far--not with a hand out, but a hand up.

*** 

About this time a plan for Sabbaticals and Educational Leaves was instituted, very much in keeping with the church's philosophy of enhancing the well-being and efficiency of its ministers. This movement began with a major innovation of granting housing allowances to all future ministers upon the sale of the two parsonages in 1971 and 1973.

In 1975 John Fulton was appointed business manager with instructions to promote economy and more freedom from routine tasks for the staff. The Priorities Task Force steered a building program toward renovation with plans to improve the kitchen and dining room, including a new rug and a storage area.  The final adopted plans were designed by Darrell Dobertin, Brent McRae and Jane Linder.  Sally Bermudes and Tom Reardon thereafter coordinated all color schemes and decorations.

## Printing the First Color Church Directory

Uplifting changes came about during these years that included brighter church interiors and the gradual introduction of colorful banners in the sanctuary. With color apparent everywhere, a new picture church directory for the first time was printed in color. Other changes included the new historical display cabinet placed in the Fellowship Room.  Emphasis was placed on interdenominational while two weekly Bible study groups began meeting on weekdays.

It was a wonderful time in the church's history with an influx of new members under forty representing 52% of the congregation it seemed appropriate to look forward to a promising future as the church moved toward the 1980s.

William Crawford, Joyce Caravetta, Sylvia Aust, Isabelle Francis, James Thrash, Nina Woomert, Peggy Evens and Elizabeth Richey, all gifted music directors, led choirs of adults, teenagers, youngsters and cherubs from1961 until 1979. Under their leadership, the music provided by the choirs was outstanding.  Even when it came to the organ, the organists urged more richness from the new organ and the church was able to spread its joy through music.

# Constitutional By-Laws Changed

In 1972 the original Constitution and By-Laws for the Irondequoit United Church of Christ was revised and amended. The following is a reprint of Article 2 and Article 4.

### Article 2. PURPOSE

The purpose of this church shall be to bind together followers of Jesus Christ to worship God, to preach the gospel of Jesus Christ, and to celebrate the sacraments; to realize Christian fellowship; and to make God's will dominant in the lives of all men.

### Article 4. DOCTRINE

This church acknowledges Jesus Christ as its sole head. It recognizes the Bible as the sufficient rule of faith and practice, and holds that living in accordance with the teachings of Jesus Christ is the true test of fellowship. Each member shall have the undisturbed right to follow the word of god according to the dictates of his own conscience under the enlightenment of the Holy Spirit. The following statement of faith, therefore, is not a test but an expression of the spirit in which the church interprets the word of God.

**STATEMENT OF FAITH**[12]: We believe in God the Eternal Spirit, Father of our Lord Jesus Christ and our Father, and to His deeds we testify: He calls the worlds into being, creates man in His own image and sets before him the ways of life and death. He seeks in holy love to save all people from aimlessness and sin. He judges men and

---

[12] Approved by the second General Synod of the United Church of Chrst held in Oberlin, Ohio, 5-9 July 1959, and submitted to the Synods, Conferences, Associations, and Churches fo their approval and use.

nations by His righteous will declared through prophets and apostles. In Jesus Christ, the man of Nazareth, our crucified and risen Lord, He has come to us and shared our common lot, conquering sin and death and reconciling the world to Himself. He bestows upon us His Holy Spirit, creating and renewing the Church of Jesus Christ, binding in covenant faithful people of all ages, tongues, and races.

He calls us into His Church to accept the cost and joy of discipleship, to be His servants in the service of men, to proclaim the gospels to all the world and resist the powers of evil, to share in Christ's baptism and eat at His table, to join Him in His passion and victory. He promises to all who trust Him forgiveness of sins and fullness of grace, courage in the struggle for justice and peace, His presence in trial and rejoicing and eternal life in His kingdom which has no end. Blessing and honor, glory and power be unto Him. Amen.

**COVENANT:** The covenant by which this church exists as a distinct body, and which every member accepts, is as follows: Recognizing the privilege and duty of uniting ourselves for Christian fellowship, the enjoyment of Christian ordinances, the public worship of God, and the advancement of His kingdom in the world, we do now, in the sight of God and invoking His blessing, solemnly covenant and agree with each other to associate ourselves to be a church of the Lord Jesus Christ, as warranted by the word of God.

***

Christian Education was not restricted to children and youth. Excellent and resourceful programs were provided through Adult Education, and over the years many individuals came forward to lead programs. Children have always been the focus since the WCTU

Sabbath school, and in 1973 the church adopted the policy of family worship, with children leaving the sanctuary after a story and going to their Sunday school classes.

The author Louis Gunnerman in 1977 wrote in the *Shaping of the United Church of Christ*, published by the United Church Press, that "The formation of the United Church of Christ was a venture of faith, a response to a vision created out of the heritage of the past in the context of new responsibilities." He went on to say that only when church people know the beliefs, movements, and events that make up their history will they be able to accept ownership and be shaped by that history.

His words ring as true today as when he wrote them. Along with the need to understand history so that people can claim ownership is the need to reach out to others.

# Stephen Ministry Remains Strong

Started in 1975, Stephen Ministry is both a very old and a very new form of lay ministry. It is very old because it is how the first Christians cared for one another. It is personified by Stephen, the church's first deacon. Christians reached out to those in need and ministered to one another as Christ instructed them to do: "Love one another as I have loved you."

Stephen Ministers must receive fifty hours of training and preparation before beginning their care-giving work. They are supervised by Stephen Leaders. Throughout their service, Stephen Ministers receive bi-weekly supervision, continuing education, and enrichment in a variety of related subjects.

The program was very new at IUCC, building solidly on that Biblical message, through intensive training to prepare lay people to reach out and care for those experiencing problems in their lives and supplementing the pastor's care.

As a result of the increasingly turbulent world, the church embraced the Stephen Series to create involved men and women skilled in reaching other people. Working closely with Rev. Bermudes and the Rev. Thomas Schroeder, Associate Minister, the group began extending the care of the church and its pastors to the congregation helping with grief, divorce, depression, illness and other critical situations.

***

After April 1975 it was as though a light went out, leaving everyone in darkness. By April 1977, however, many have managed to escape from Vietnam. They, like hundreds of other Vietnamese who could not endure life in Communist Vietnam, took to the sea in overloaded boats. They became part of the so-called "boat people" who continue to cause so much humanitarian concern for the international community.  Some people have wondered why Vietnam fell to the Communists, particularly since it had been dedicated for the preaching of the gospel. Actually, the question is naive. Dedicatory prayers are just that—prayers, not commands. Such prayers do not impose the Lord's will on mankind; rather, they bless the efforts of the Lord's servants. In 1976 the church sponsored the Doi family from Vietnam in conjunction with the Board of Christian Outreach. The church clothed and housed the family as well as provided food. The results of the care and love led to the Doi family becoming self-supporting.

In 1977 the Rev. Bermudes' Five-Year Plan for developing an atmosphere in which warmer fellowship might bloom encouraged more neighbor group activity outside the church and fuller use of the Fellowship Room that had been formed within the space of the former chapel in 1974.

## Music Directors Kathy and Bruce Beardsley

In 1979 Kathy and Bruce Beardsley joined the Irondequoit United Church of Christ as Music Director and Organist. The quality, resourcefulness, depth and scope of music were at its peak of perfection.

There was the instrumental ensembles prepared and coached by Elizabeth and David Richey for the performance of the Messiah at Christmas in 1983.

Later there was the publishing of a new hymn supplement.

Bruce and Kathy Beardsley,
Rev. Thomas Schroeder

There was even the special month of music honoring Handel's 300th anniversary, and the 1985 musical *"David's Hotshot Slingshot,"* featuring the Junior and Chapel Choirs and Senior Choir personalities.

These were but a few of the memorable events.

In 1980 the church permanently divided its academic year into four quarters of seven weeks each.  They established three chief topics: Biblical Studies, Family and Self, and Current Issues.

That same year the Irondequoit United Church of Christ sponsored the Lmuth (La-moot) family through its Cambodian Ministry Committee. They were refugees from Cambodia in need of a sponsor to enter the United States and IUCC was more than willing to come to their aid. The request for sponsors originated with the Church World Services, which by now had grown as a cooperative ministry of thirty-five Protestant, Orthodox, and Anglican denominations, providing sustainable self-help and development, disaster relief, and refugee assistance in some eighty countries.

The United Church Board for World Ministries opened the communication channels, and the family arrived in Rochester in February 1980 via Thailand, in the hopes of beginning a better life.

The family consists of the father, Pheng, his wife Cheam Kuong (Shem Kung); the oldest daughter Maly (Maw-lee'), the second oldest daughter, Phea (Pe'-oh) and the youngest daughter Phao (Pow). Care and arrangements to help them adjust to their new country continued for the family until they moved to St. Paul, Minnesota.

## Dedication Of The Memorial Chapel

A new chapel, accommodating thirty-five chairs and an organ from the earlier larger chapel, was installed in the old stage room. Stained-glass windows were designed and built by Brent McRae, and Dorothy and Fred Kunkel and Charter Member Harriet McCullough gave furnishings in memory of Homer Smith and charter member Ida Smith. At the same time, the Fellowship Room received a face lift and was refurbished with a historical display cabinet. A symbolic icon, "The Tree of Life," a gift of Dorothy and Fred Kunkel, graced the south side, resplendent in light green leaves and golden boughs.

The following comes from the program for the Service of Dedication of the Memorial Chapel. " Held on Sunday, September 21, 1980, at nine o'clock. The Introduction was given by Rev. Robert W. Bermudes. The Litany of Dedication was led by John Titus, Ruth Elmemdorf, Harriett McCullough, Dorothy Kunkel and Fred Kunkel. The Prayer of Dedication was led by Rev. Richard Grobe."

At the bottom of the program was this notation:

"A list of all Gifts and Memorials which have been made to the Irondequoit United Church of Christ will be found in a permanent recording of all Memorials and Special Gifts inscribed in the 'Abiding Memorials' which is on display in the Chapel."

The back page of the program contained the following history:

*"The area dedicated today as a chapel was in actual fact the "stage room" in the auditorium of the Sunday school sponsored by the Women's Christian Temperance Union from 1885 until the completion of the present meeting house in 1926. At that time the auditorium was converted into a chapel and the stage was walled off to make a small meeting room. In 1973 it was*

*decided to convert the chapel into a Fellowship Room to accommodate Sunday morning coffee hours, small classes and meetings, and a better traffic pattern for people entering and leaving the building. However, once more there was no chapel, and the frequent requests for small weddings, funerals, and a quiet meditation area, led the Memorial Committee to underwrite the cost of the structural renovations to make this room possible. Provision for the furnishings has been made by generous gifts from charter member Harriett McCullough, in memory of her mother, Lillie Cole, also a charter member, and from Dorothy and Fred Kunkel, in memory of charter member Ida Smith and her husband, Homer Smith, Dorothy's parents."*

At the outset of the project, the Memorial Committee sought designs from the Merkel Donohue Company, whose decorating recommendations have been incorporated throughout in concert with changes made to the Fellowship Room at the same time. The Henry Yeager Construction, Inc accomplished the structural changes.

A member of this church, Brent McRae, whose devoted attention to detail and color produced the remarkable stories in glass, constructed the four stained glass windows. Each flame relates an important Christian concept; the single large star speaks of Jesus' birth; the dove reminds us of the baptism of Jesus by water and the Holy Spirit; the flame wrapped about the cross symbolizes the fire of the Holy Spirit at Pentecost; and the bread and wine suggest Christ's continuing communion with his people.

The Stained Glass Windows In The Chapel

There was a memorable notation on the cover of the program:

*There are varieties of gifts,*
*but the same spirit.*
*There are varieties of*
*service, but the same Lord.*
*In each of us the Spirit is*
*manifested in one particular*
*way, for some useful*
*purpose.*
*And together we are the*
*Body of Christ."*

In 1981 Boy Scout Troop 154 celebrated its thirty-year anniversary. The troop was active in all phases of Scouting right from the start. The Boy Scouts of America as one of the nation's largest values-based youth development organization making it a perfect fit to IUCC principles, with their programs designed to build character, train in the responsibilities of participating citizenship, and develop personal fitness.

A pattern of interesting programs that included camping and companionship continued through the years with success being measured in many ways. Five hundred and fifty-five boys were in

Troop 154 over the thirty years, with eighty-five active scouts registered at that time.

The Peacemaking Task Force began in early 1983 under the leadership of Sally Bermudes. It was active in supporting nuclear disarmament and encouraged study and regular communication with representatives in Washington, D.C. Later the name would be changed to the Peacemaking Focus Group.

In 1983 Elizabeth and David Richey prepared and coached the performance of the Messiah at Christmas and by 1983 Christian Education was not restricted to children and youth. Excellent and resourceful programs were provided by the Adult Education Committee, which was led by Gary Leubner.

In 1984 the Social Concerns Committee began to study in depth and act on the issues of hunger, aging, sanctuary, and aid to refugees.

## Opening Our Building To Others

Reaching out mingled with fun with the Living Christmas Card Carol.  Songs were sung in the snow on the church steps in 1983 and again in 1984. By this time many organizations and services met in the building, including the Grange, Autistic Children, Antiquarian Group, Boy Scouts, Girl Scouts, Community Nursery School, Genesee Valley Association of the UCC, Literacy Volunteers, Irondequoit Forum, Red Cross Disaster Training, Weight Watchers, and Alcoholics Anonymous.

Sponsorship of the Girl Scouts of Genesee Valley, Inc. by the Irondequoit United Church of Christ was made official in October of 1984 when they signed an agreement of sponsorship.

## TIE LINE OF LOVE

In May and June of 1985 the church's three-channel **TIE LINE OF LOVE** was created. Three constant telephone ministries were conducted daily over three channels. The first, **Prayer Line,** provided inspiration and thoughtful prayers by one of the pastors. **Story Line** provided an eight-minute Bible story telling. The **Help Line** was for pertinent and perceptive messages by expert professional counselors who dealt with topics such as aging, marriage, addiction, and individual loss. To get the word out, a schedule appeared in *"The Lighted Cross"* and was distributed to nursing homes and other outlets. At its heyday, 1400 calls came into the channels each month.

In November 1985 the church voted to be a Sanctuary Support Church, which required a promise to contribute to the financial support of the Rochester Sanctuary Committee.

## VISCOM Is Five Years Old

Dan Reardon With The VISCOM Members Setting Up A Slide Show

That year also marked the fifteenth anniversary of VISCOM (Visual Communications), formerly known as Action Moviemaking. VISCOM continued to offer students a unique means of expression through photography, videography and music.  Under the masterful direction of Don Reardon the group grew in size and knowledge and Don continued as the VISCOM leader.

To celebrate this landmark, the group presented a historical review in movies and slides of the previous fifteen years.  In 1986, VISCOM received an award for its slide show entitled "The River Story." Western New York Chapter presented the award for the Association for Multi-Image, in conjunction with their annual student night. VISCOM was an outgrowth of the earlier film-making group, which won two U.N. awards and has gone on to emphasize the use of contemporary forms of communication. In its earliest days in the seventies, the group was headed by Henry Schwede, followed by Richard Grobe and then Dan Reardon, a graduate of RIT's School of Photography.

In April 1985 two slow-action ceiling fans were installed in the sanctuary that both reduced heating costs by nearly twenty per cent and helped to offset the summer heat. A few months following, in September, a new, extensive loop induction system, which functions through hearing aids and otherwise, purchased with individual gifts to the Memorial Fund, was designed and added to the sanctuary's acoustic apparatus to forestall individual difficulties in hearing during the service.

## Outreach Continued To Grow

The IUCC continued with its past outreach programs and added on many more.

The **UCC Hunger Fund**: In partnership with the United Church of Christ and the Christian Church (Disciples of Christ), Foods Resource Bank responded to the problem of world hunger and helped hungry people know the dignity and pride of feeding themselves.

**Back Bay Mission of Biloxi, Mississippi**: Back Bay Mission was founded in 1922. Members responded with compassion and service to the needs of poor "fisher folk." Back Bay Mission has continually grown and, although there were no longer any UCC congregations in Biloxi or in the state of Mississippi by the early 1970s, Back Bay Mission remained. Its commitment is to be faithfully responsive to the emerging and critical needs of God's people, ever seeking a day of greater justice and peace.

**Charles Hall Home for Indian Youths (Bismarck, North Dakota)**: Since its early beginnings in 1965, Charles Hall Youth Services has strived to meet the needs of at-risk youth in a holistic way, working toward healing and strengthening youth emotionally, mentally, physically and spiritually. The agency is committed to integrating spirituality with therapeutic practices, building on existing skills and mental health specialties to include the spiritual dimension.

**Emmanus Home for Retarded Adults, Pennsylvania**: The Emmaus Community of Pittsburgh serves persons with developmental disabilities and mental retardation by offering a wide range of programs and services including quality residential housing. Another important aspect of their mission is to effectively educate the public about the unique needs and issues of people with mental retardation and developmental disabilities and advocate for a heightened response to those needs. At the heart of their mission to serve is love.

The **G.V.A. (Genesee Valley Association) Memorial Fund**, Women out of Prison, and other local and distant activisms were also part of Outreach involvement.

The many fun times included the Living Christmas Card Carol Sings in the snow on the church steps in 1983 and 1984. The church overnights in the fall at Camp Onanda and Camp Stella Maris, along with picnics at Seneca Park with outdoor worship, a family picnic and outdoor sports.

The church was growing and changing. In October and November of 1985 at a special church meeting, IUCC voted to be a "Sanctuary Support Church" following the presentation of the Sanctuary Education Series.

The *Reflections* book marking the seventy-five year birthday of Irondequoit United Church of Christ stated that the church was built in the market place. The fields and market gardens it once overlooked are now an ever-growing complex of shopping malls and parking lots, an aspect of the suburb that became prosperous and more plastic each year. The church described in its earlier history now stares at the former Grange Hall that become a famed youth and music cult emporium. The eleven saloons, challenged and soundly rebuked by the WCTU founders, are gone, but so much of the bustling world is at the church doors that its front entrance is now only discreetly opened.

The days when the church buildings were next to the high school and when the fields to the north were used for football practice are difficult to remember. Marketplace or not, future historians who study the environs of Rochester will be amazed at the enlightenment that has emanated from the plot of ground at the corner of Cooper Road and Titus Avenue. Good schools there have benefited the children since Civil War days, but the institution that has done so much to enhance the quality of life in West Irondequoit for the past seventy-five years and that will enlarge us incalculably in the years to come is the United Church of Christ.

## Seventy-Five Years And Onward

The seventy-five-year mark for IUCC came after hundreds of babies, 1,500 weddings, 4,000 burials, and 3,900 sermons given by dozens of pastors.

The Jubilee Year of our sanctuary took place on October 17, 1986, coinciding with the Bicentennial year of our nation.  The day began with the worship service at which the congregation was asked to come dressed in colonial costumes and participate in a service much as it might have been 200 years ago.  The service was in the manner and dress of the 18th century Congregationalists from whom we had derived our polity.  There were plays on the history of our church and its founders, along with displays of historical memorabilia.

Model of the 1911 Church Building
Designed by Patricia Partridge
Constructed by Effie Partridge
of the Ruth Circle.
Figures supplied by Helen Allen

The Anniversary Worship Service program book was distinctive.  The inside pages appear below.  Words that seem misspelled are exactly as they appeared in this program.

| |
|---|
| **ANNIVERSARY WORSHIP SERVICE** |
| (after the manner of the New England Congregational Churches prior |

to the American Revolution)

**DRUMMING TO WORSHIP**       Mr. Hermie Dressel, Drummer

(The original meeting house in what is now known as "Smalley" or "Paradise" park had neither bell nor belfry.  Instead, as was customary in Colonial days, a drummer from the local company summoned the congregation to worship in the military manner.)

**ENTRANCE OF THE MINISTERS**

(It was reported that when Dr. Smalley entered the great front door of the meetinghouse, he gave a little stamp of the foot, which was the signal for the elders and principal men to rise as he passed along the broad aisle to the pulpit.  In many churches the approach of the minister was signaled by a rap of the tithingman's stick.)

**OPENING PRAYER**

(It was the overwhelming conviction of the early Congregationalists that "free prayers" and not "stinted forms" were the most acceptable form of worship to god.  This was taken to such an extreme that they would not even allow the Lord's Prayer to be used in worship, regarding this as a pattern rather than as a formula of prayer.)

THE SINGING OF A PSALM (Hymn No 1)        Mr. Fredric Schmalz, Precentor

(Music in the Colonial churches was confined exclusively to the singing of psalms without accompaniment.  By 1758, however, instruments were beginning to be introduced into the churches, the commonest being the cello, usually called "God's fiddle" as opposed to the "Devil's fiddle", the violin, used at dances and secular affairs.  This and the pitch pipe are probably the "Instrewments of musick" for singing".  There being but a limited supply of printed Psalters, the psalms were "lined out" by a precentor while those who had attended one of the informal "singing schools" set up from time to time in various communities stood in a single row along the railing of the back balcony and led the singing while the congregation remained seated.)

**THE READING AND EXPOSITION OF THE SCRIPTURES**

         The Rev. Robert W. Bermudes

(Our Congregational forerunners disapprove of what they called the "dumb" reading of scripture, i.e., reading without comment and explanation as was customary in the Church of England, and insisted that whole chapters rather than brief "lessons", must be read with immediate exposition.)

THE SINGING OF A PSALM (Hymn No. 86)

**THE PASTORAL PRAYER**     The Rev. Edward C. Dahl

(Responses were definitely omitted both as reminders of the liturgical and therefore unbiblical worship of the Roman and Anglican churches and on the basis that God had forbidden the cuckoo as meat for the Israelites!)

**THE BRINGING OF THE OFFERING**

OFFERTORY ANTHEM:  "Rejoice in the Lord, Always"        Henry Purcell

As the church reviewed its past and declared its future in 1986, three quarters of a century after its beginning in the Irondequoit WCTU Hall, they continued witnessing Christ, worshiping Christ, serving Christ, meeting in fellowship with Christ and each other, nurturing ourselves and our children as intelligently as we can, and reaching out in Christ as far and as fittingly as we can.

Both of our 1986 Easter services were made special by the addition to the fellowship music performers, the Chi Rho Bell Choir, trained and led by the Beardsley's.

The Chi Rho Choir was then made up of artists of all ages including some young people. There were now nearly two concert choirs of trained, skillful bell ringers ready for performances.

CHORUS LINE

SUNDAY, APRIL 27

Worship          11:00
Dinner           12:00
Program           1:30


Want a chuckle?  Want a grin?

Come and see the "State" you're in!

The Chorus Line is after lunch.....

Plan ahead and join the bunch!

Sparkle, wit and info, too,

This All Star Line-up is for You!!!

A Cast of 22

It was nicely put when printed in the program: "The past has not all vanished. Many of the things the Church does—most of what it has and much of what it is—are inheritances, held in trust to conserve."

At the 75-year mark, the Rev. Robert W. Bermudes was the pastor and the Rev. Thomas M. Schroeder the Associate Minister. Mr. Bruce Beardsley, Organist, and Mrs. Kathleen Beardsley, Music Director. The church reported a decrease in membership and in church attendance which also lead to a diminishing amount in pledges. To curve this downward trend, the Futuring Committee was formed

CHI RHO
BELL CHOIR

JUNIOR CHOIR

CHAPEL CHOIR

SENIOR
CHOIR

For seventy-five years the Irondequoit United Church of Christ provided ministry at the same location on Titus Avenue. Seventy-five years passed with only two living charter members, Grace Slater and Aura Bable, who were honored at the seventy-five-year celebration.

Just as important to the success of the church were the dedicated committee members who spent months designing a celebration –"Seventy-Five Years and Onward"—that represented what the church meant to its members.  Their job was to lay out the framework for the upcoming events that would meet the standards of the celebrations that had gone on before, and with the support of the church body they succeeded in making the year memorable for all. The seventy-fifth-year celebration of the church was called "*75 Years and Onward.*"

## "75 And Onward" Committee

R. Bermudes, P. Stanton, H. Hulse, D. Killip,  M. Thorne, M. Casey, T. Schroeder
M. Hopper, D. Kunkel, B. Stanton, E. Partridge
Not Present:  E. Miller,  H. Klein and M. Gibson

Preparations done by Ruth Circle started long before the plans were in place. This group saw to the creation of a quilt for the 75th celebration.  With Jane Linder serving as the sewing organizer, a masterpiece was created and ready in time for the celebration.

**Quilt Made For The 1986**

Customs prevailed as they planned the traditional lighting of the candles, the traditional services and dinner.  There were three celebrations: one for the **PAST** held, in February, one for the **PRESENT**, held in April, and one for the **FUTURE**, held in November.

The series began with Noah's family, portrayed with puppets, rainbows and an ark handmade and hand-worked by the children. They also presented stars for the year 2011 for the celebration of the church's 100th year.

The Three Covenants marked the last in the series of three ceremonies celebrating the anniversary.

The rainbow seen above Noah's Ark was a work of joy and pride Worship and singing played an important role in the celebration. The talents were never-ending

The Noah's Ark Created By The Children

The Noah's Ark Rainbow For 75th

**Decorations Were Many
For the 75th Celebration**

**The Presentation By The Choir**

Replicas of our church were hand crafted by Effie and Pat Partridge and, of course, what would a birthday be without the cake?

Effie Partridge, serving as the chairman of the Decorations Committee, discussed the history of the candle lighting.

> *Fifty years earlier, on March 8, 1936, on the 25th anniversary of the United Congregational Church, a candle-lighting service was held to commemorate the origin and development of the church. Mrs. Polly Rogers Hunt, a charter member, lighted the candle. Twenty-five years earlier, in 1961, the candle-lighting service tradition was preserved at the 50th anniversary. On the 75th year, they again lighted candles to honor their beginnings and, symbolically, to light their way into the future.*

Polly Frazier, niece of Polly Rogers Hunt, in honor and remembrance of the dedicated women who organized the Women's Christian Temperance Union and the first Sabbath School, lighted the first candle.

The second candle was lighted by Grace Slater, charter member, in honor and remembrance of the founders of the church.

The third candle was lighted by Megan Smith to symbolize the future.

***

At the end of seventy-five years and with the formation of a Futuring Committee, the need was expressed to increase membership. Pledges were low, leaving the church with a critical shortfall.  The church needed to direct energies, generosity and cooperative efforts to take an upward climb. The Futuring Committee, formed in September 1983, called in a church consultant who, in consultation with the Committee, created the Walrath Report (named after the consultant) in June of 1984. Based on interviews and observation, the seventeen-page report listed concerns and significant problem areas with suggestions for corrections. It was hoped that, armed with the analysis of IUCC, the church could discover a way to overcome the problems of the past that had led to membership loss and pledges.

The year's top story was the tragic loss of the NASA space shuttle Challenger and the deaths of all seven persons aboard.  The early months of 1986 brought good economic news.  The Federal Reserve dropped its discount interest rate to 7% and finally to 6% by midyear.  Prices fell by a record amount and consumer prices were down for the first time in years.  The bad news was that unemployment was still rising and factory production was down.

Not immune to the economical changes of the world, IUCC still struggled onward.  As the years progressed, the Irondequoit United Church of Christ kept finding more ways to reach out to the community. From their community participation in ventures such as the CROP Walk, the annual Strawberry Festival, the Christmas season's "Sermon in Music" the church continued its level of giving and receiving from the community.

The tradition of the quilt-making also remained a stable part of the church's past and present history.  By this time the quilts were a tradition that every member enjoyed.  Anticipations were high as the centennial year approached.  From the 25 year quilt to the 75 year quilt, all wondered what the theme of the 100 year quilt would be.

The church had a membership of 938 on the church rolls, but on the average in 1988 only 206 members were present on Sundays. Attendance was a problem being faced by many churches of all denominations, who also issued studies to understand the cause of congregational membership decline and how to seek recovery of congregational health. The causes of the numerical decline involved issues relating to rural and urban life, demographics, societal change, congregational health, mission and vision.

Studies show that congregations that grow and are vital in the Christian mission have several things in common. They are healthy, have relevant ministries, they consider growth a high priority, they are inviting and welcoming to newcomers and they are mission-, not maintenance-orientated. The question then was how to reverse the spiral of decline while keeping in mind that the church needed more than just large numbers of people attending church. Numbers can be important, but they do not tell the whole story, nor are they an indication of genuine faith. A lack of numbers does pose a threat to the long-term health of the denomination and is certainly one indicator of spiritual health.

# Churches Uniting

The 1988 New York State Conference Quilt

In 1988 the New York State Conference was held in June, and for the event a quilt was made that presented a message. This was a very special quilt indeed as one hundred New York State churches contributed an original quilt square based on the theme "Hospitality."

The squares were sewn together for a backdrop for the conference that was held in Cortland, New York and for the Irondequoit United Church of Christ, Ruth MacGregor is credited with making the quilt square.

As part of the joint effort of United Churches of Christ, the Just Peace initiative was born. This, described in detail by UCC states that what "Just Peace" Means to Us is courage in the struggle for justice and peace. This is central to the identity of our church; one of our most ardent prayers and richest blessings. To be part of the United Church of Christ is to be part of the struggle for justice and peace. In June of 1985, the Fifteenth General Synod of the United Church of Christ took two important actions to strengthen this identity. They declared Justice and Peace to be a priority of the church for the next four years, and they passed a Pronouncement "Affirming the United Church of Christ to be a Just Peace Church." The Synod then called on local churches and conferences to organize their common life so as to make a difference in the achieving of a Just Peace and the ending of the institution of war. In 1989, the priority for a Just Peace was extended to include environmental concerns and was called the priority for Integrity of Creation, Justice and Peace.

In April of 1989, the Just Peace Church Education Series took place in May at the annual meeting, and the IUCC voted to be a "*Just Peace Church*." It was then that the Just Peace Focus Group began. Declaring ourselves a Just Peace Church was not an unprecedented move. This action was a recognition of our identity as a congregation already concerned with God's call to be peacemakers and a statement of our determination to be more intentional in our worship, programs and activities to develop our identity as a Just Peace Church.  It was later called the **Earthcare Focus Group**.

***

In 1989, after nine years of service to IUCC, the Beardsley's announced they were stepping down as Music Director and Organist. They had done so much to enhance the music and worship life of IUCC that it became hard to fathom anyone being capable of filling their shoes. Yet the gift of the Beardsley's continued with the introduction of Jane Brinkman. Ms. Brinkman was determined and successful in making a wonderful transition into the music and organist position of IUCC and soon her presence was accepted and cherished as a welcome addition to the service.

Still more changes were to come, and some were refreshing. For instance, through the generosity of many, a third octave of bells was purchased. The result was a richer, fuller sound heard on Sundays when the Bell Choir performed.

A handbell choir is a group that rings music with melodies and harmony. The bells used generally include all notes of the chromatic scale within the range of the bell set. There are two octaves  sets as well as larger, ranging up to a seven-and-a-half-octave set. The bells are arranged chromatically on foam-covered tables; these tables protect the bronze surface of the bell, as well as keep the bells from rolling when placed on their sides. Unlike an orchestra or choir in which each musician is responsible for one line of the texture, a bell ensemble acts as one instrument, with each musician responsible for particular notes, sounding his or her assigned bells whenever that note appears in the music.

To show how much the new bells were appreciated, a dedication service for the third octave was held in June with both the Chi Rho and Chapel Choirs ringing.

## The Memorial Garden

Another pleasant change came from another direction. An appeal was made by Robert Bermudes concerning the Memorial Garden.

Rev. Bermudes stated that a church member had approached him with an earnest request. The church member informed Rev. Bermudes that they no longer had any local family beyond the church, nor did they wish to purchase a plot for their burial. Instead it was their desire to be with the church family. The request was for burial in the memorial garden.

The Memorial Garden was in between the buildings of the United Church and the space was in view from the walkway to the Sanctuary.

Our Memorial Garden

Churches are communities of memory and hope. We know that we are part of a pilgrimage through time that began long before us and continues long after us. This garden represented a respect for those pilgrims who preceded us. It was also a gift to future generations. From the first, this garden was intended to be a place of remembrance and contemplation. The fact that it was located in the enclosed area it was a constant reminder of the progression of the generations. This new purpose would remind us that life goes on. It would keep fresh in memory that we are recipients of a great gift, the gift of life, which is to be cherished.

Christian churches have been associated with cemeteries for centuries, so why not a burying ground in our memorial garden? .With the approval of the congregation, a meeting was held to determine how to go about this. The conclusions were that there would be no markings on the ground of the individualized plots; each would be carefully numbered and laid out in a map grid of twelve-inch squares. The plantings would be carefully removed and replaced for each committal. They determined there would be room for as many as sixty-five plots.

The memorial garden had a new purpose with each cremains encapsulated in PVC containers.  Each location was clearly listed with the name and recorded on a plaque at the entrance to the garden.

***

The reach of the Irondequoit United Church of Christ went out into the world when they voted to become one of the six churches in the area offering to provide sanctuary to Guatemalan and Salvadoran refugees.  The incident that sparked this interest came about on November 16, 1989, when Ms. Elba Julia Ramos and her daughter Celina were killed by U.S.-backed Salvadoran government troops, for having worked for the Jesuit priests of the University of Central America where they were witnesses to their assassination. Among the slain priests was Dr. Ignacio Martin-Baro, a tireless human-rights advocate who had an intense commitment to the liberation of women and supplied critical data for the research presented here.

The nationwide sanctuary movement included more than 230 churches, synagogues, student associations and cities that offered transportation, housing, food and other types of aid to the refugees. The goal was to send a message to the Reagan administration that the refugees should be granted political asylum.  For its role, The Irondequoit United Church of Christ offered both financial and moral assistance.

***

In 1989 IUCC saw an increase in attendance to 230, and by 1990 the average attendance was up to 270.  Though the congregation had decreased significantly over the years from its heyday at over 1000, this improvement was looked upon as a stepping stone in the right direction.

It was around this time that Mrs. Ruth MacGregor presented the Bonnie Blue Star Quilt to the Church Historian, Dorothy Kunkel, so that it could be displayed at the 100th IUCC Anniversary Celebrations

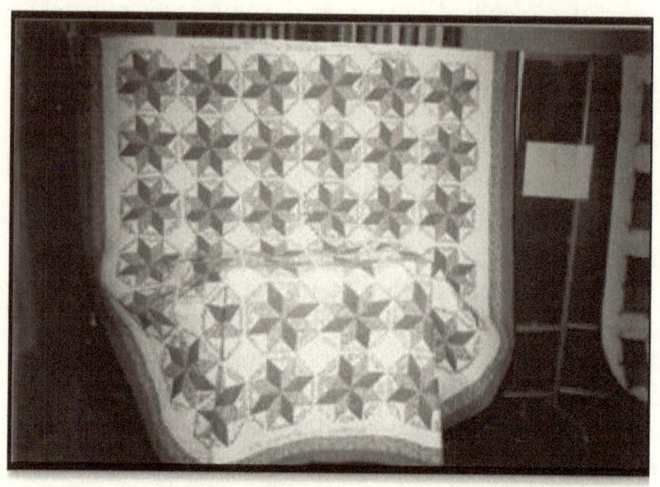

BONNIE BLUE QUILT MADE IN 1936

## The Sunset House

Among the changes to come about in 1989 was our outreach to Sunset House. The Sunset House is a home for the dying located in Irondequoit. The home was founded in 1990 by Jim and Gail Nealon after the passing of their 16 year old daughter Jennifer.

The Nealons committed themselves to establishing a local residence where those with an end stage illness could receive dignified comfort care in a homelike setting. Sunset House became a hospice to provide care that involves health professionals and dedicated volunteers for medical, emotional and spiritual support. By the end of that summer, Sunset House was operational and IUCC was there to provide assistance in any means necessary.

# The Peace Pole

In April of 1990, on Earth Day, a dogwood tree was planted by the parking lot door, and in May the Irondequoit United Church of Christ conveyed a message of peace by placing a Peace Pole in front of the church.

The peace pole says, *"May Peace Prevail on Earth"* inscribed in four languages: English, Russian, Spanish, and Seneca. Its purpose is to act as a constant reminder of the necessity to work and pray for peace at all times.

The Peace Pole Project was started in Japan in 1976 by the Society for World Peace, and since then more than 65,000 peace poles have been dedicated the world over as international symbols of peace.

**August of 1996, The Earthcare Focus Group**

The Peace Pole Inscription In Four Languages

The Peace Pole, seated from left are Teresa Bermudes and Denae McDonald
Standing:  from left, Sally Bermudes, Babs Reimensnyder and Randy McDonald

# Endowment Fund

An IUCC Endowment Fund was created to provide a means for members and friends of the church to continue to support the programs on a permanent basis. The Endowment Committee was established by the Endowment Fund Charter, adopted in February of 1990. The Committee began operations in mid 1990 with the responsibility of managing the Fund for the benefit of IUCC's general programs:

| | |
|---|---|
| The St. Paul Legacy To Humanity Fund | Supports Special Outreach Programs |
| The Grace Slater Fund | Benefits The Church School |
| The Archie Groth Fund | Supports Stephen Ministry. |

***

In 1992 the Senior Citizens Fun Club was in full swing, meeting the first Monday of each month for lunch and activities. Each member brought a sandwich and table settings, with drinks and dessert supplied. Members paid a $2.00 yearly membership fee and a $1 charge to cover the cost of dessert. Such fun events as slide shows of travels, valentine parties, pot luck suppers, guest speakers and a yearly Christmas party were just a few of the planned events.

In November of 1992, the "*Christian Nonviolence Retreat*" was led by Father Emmanuel Charles McCarthy, sponsored by the *Peacemaking Focus Group*. Then in 1993 Rev. Bermudes reported on the formation of an Alzheimer's Support Group started by Stephen Ministers. Along with Rev. Bermudes, Herb Humphrey hoped to encourage members to entertain the idea of this new group for ministry.

This was also the year of a big news story that ran for almost a week. Described as one of the largest and most intense storms in a century, the March 12-14, 1993 blizzard paralyzed the eastern seaboard with record cold, snow, and wind.

The combined effects of wind and heavy wet snow downed thousands of miles of power lines leaving millions of people in the dark for up to a week.  The blizzard of '93, as it is known in the Northeast or Superstorm '93 as it is known elsewhere is considered one of the all time most intense storms to have formed over and affected such a large portion of the United States. Beforehand, fearing the worst, Rochesterians went out in droves to prepare. The media could not agree on when the storm would hit. Some reports claimed light snow would start around late afternoon; others said it would not hit until much later at night. When it finally arrived, the storm, called a white hurricane, had some of the deepest snows of the region: 36 inches in Syracuse, 27 inches in Albany, 23 in Rochester, 22 in Binghamton and Schenectady, 30 in Elmira, 24 in Troy and 18 in Buffalo.  The blizzard would remind us of how our ancestry lived before the invent of electricity and other comforts.  It was indeed a testament to survival and the ability to overcome obstacles.  This reminder was soon to hit a personal tone in the Irondequoit United Church of Christ.

***

More than 450 people gathered on a Sunday in June of 1993 at IUCC to hear Rev. Bermudes deliver his final sermon. It had been twenty years since the first time he had stood before the church, and the congregation came on this day to hear his final words and to say goodbye to their minister, their friend.  Rev. Bermudes was retiring as the pastor of IUCC. He said that in looking back on his career he hoped people would remember him as an "effective preacher and minister,

one who took a stand on issues and who applied a social gospel mission
of caring."

By the end of 1994, average attendance for the year was down
to 197, which could be accounted to Rev. Bermudes' resignation.  As
the books closed on 1994, there was considerable satisfaction on the
performance of the U.S. economy. Over the past year, economic
growth increased by close to 4 percent; and led to impressive
employment gains. The economy created over 3 million new jobs in
1994, including over a quarter million new manufacturing jobs. These
job gains, led to a significant drop in the unemployment rate to the
lowest level in four years.

The strength in the U.S. economy was broad-based among both
consumers and businesses. A final highlight of 1994 was the
performance of inflation. Despite indications of tightening labor
markets and increased materials prices, inflation remained under
control

***

The Rev. Ken Whitwer of Michigan, who came with his wife,
Judy, was installed as Interim Minister, but change always results in an
unsettling of the congregation and during the same year, the Associate
Pastor, Cheryl Huff Slusser, announced that she, too, would be leaving.
Unsettled but determine to make the best of the situation, the
Irondequoit United Church of Christ went forward with searching for a
new pastor, not allowing the change to have any adverse affects on the
programs and people of the congregation, knowing that pastoral
transitions due to resignations or retirements are a common event in the
life of the church. The emotions and stress levels surrounding pastoral
transitions are anything but common but eventually a pastor will
announce that he/she is going to accept a new call either to another
church or to retirement. Such news is always comes as somewhat of a
shock. With the help of Rev. Ken Whitwer, Interim Pastor, the process
began to help the congregation understand what an emotionally
powerful time it is for both himself as Interim Pastor and for
congregational members so he encouraged open communication on the
subject.  Pastoral good-byes are a time to celebrate what is best about
the body of Christ.

The Sanctuary As It Was In 1995

***

The Stephen Lay Ministry program continued during 1995, but the level of activity was not as great as it had been in past years, so to stimulate interest, a training class for new Stephen Lay Ministers was conducted during the fall of 1995.

The group tackled environmental, peace and justice issues, and as laypeople and Stephen Ministers to care for others within our congregation. The 1999 Stephen Ministers appear in the picture that follows.

| Waltraud Englemann | Ann Smith | Maggie Ritchey | Marjorie Case |

# Rev. Jerry Alan Smith (1995-2000

In April of 1995, the church welcomed the Rev. Jerry Alan
Smith and his wife, Cheryl C. Smith, as the new minister of the church.
Rev. Bermudes had served as our pastor since 1972 and this was indeed
the longest period of time that one pastor had remained (21 years).
Only two other ministers remained beyond ten years and that was Rev.
Charles S. Bergner (17 years) and Rev. Lloyd Stamp. (11 years).  The
church members needed to deal with their feelings about the resigning
of Rev. Bermudes and begin to look ahead.  Being ready to commit to
new pastoral leadership is an important task at this time, but by the time
Rev. Jerry Alan was hired as the new pastor of the Irondequoit United
Church of Christ, the church body was ready.

***

In the early 80s, the medical world was just beginning to study
a new disease that created mysterious and fatal symptoms.  Acquired
Immune Deficiency Syndrome or Acquired Immunodeficiency
Syndrome (AIDS) is an infection resulting from the damage to the
human immune system.

IUCC members who participated in AIDS walk included from the left front row: Chris Quinlan, Eleanor Fike, Babs Reimensnyder, Sherie Lindamood, Left rear: Ann Cunningham, Barbara Saner and Deb Sponable

AIDS had claimed the lives of millions of people and it was anticipated that by the year 2000, approximately eight million would have died as a result of AIDS and approximately 40 million would be infected with the virus that caused AIDS.

Each day, six thousand people acquired the AIDS virus. Women and teens were being infected in record numbers. Something this big required the grace of God, so IUCC stepped up and participated in the AIDS Walk, raising $2,300 for the cause.

***

Keeping with the tradition of remembering the past, in 1997 a Mother-Daughter Banquet was put on by Women's Fellowship. Although this event had become a tradition over the past years, this one had a special twist. For this banquet, members of Women's Fellowship provided wedding gowns. Some of the dresses were worn by their owners, and others were modeled by members of the congregation. The event was a success, with each bride being escorted along the center aisle of the church for all to see.

The joy of the words, "Ahh the good old days" was apparent on many faces. The music, the sights, the sounds of a place that we can never fully recapture was being revisited. These memories of times past was nostalgic to many as they watched and remembered, with that warm glow feeling witnessed on many faces.

The church's ministry continued to grow and  in 1997 included
the Material Aids group.  The Material Aids Group supplies
quilts, school kits and baby kits for the Church World Service
(CWS) to distribute to people in need throughout the world.
Members meet monthly to make "gifts of the heart" - they tie
quilts and cut squares for at-home quilt sewing, knit and/or sew

baby sweaters for baby kits and school bags for school kits.  The project specifications are provided in detail by Church World Services so that the each recipient will receive the same.  CWS collects all materials annually for worldwide distribution from their Maryland facility.  The Material Aids group of IUCC set the third Wednesday morning of each month for their meetings

In June of 1998, long-time Church Historian, Dorothy Smith Kunkel, passed.  She was a member of the church for fifty-eight years, and her mother and aunt were charter members. In her honor, her husband, Fred Kunkel, donated the funds to renovate the Fellowship Room in her memory.  Ann Smith would step up to become the next historian.

# The Irondequoit Ministerial Association

In 1999 approximately two hundred people from a dozen churches in Irondequoit came together to focus on unity and launched a joint project.

The Irondequoit Ministerial Association coordinated the ecumenical Week of Prayer for a Christian Unity worship service on a Sunday afternoon at IUCC.  The Rev. Jerry Alan Smith, Rochester Mayor William Johnson, the Rev. Sarah Greenfield and the Rev. Frank Harahan sang hymns together. The service reminded those present that there is great hope that Christians may soon bring about reconciliation among those who believe in Christ, in spite of the hindrance of many historical, theological, cultural, and psychological obstacles.

It was stated that it seemed we had not yet discovered the means for breaking down the barriers that still divided us and impeded a unified proclamation of the gospel to the world. To walk together,

Christians need to be grounded in the Word of God, the revelation of God's face in Jesus Christ, the renewing force of God's Spirit, the discovery of the love of God, Father, Son and Holy Spirit. Without light from the source of all light, the problems we encounter on our way remain shrouded in darkness and become insurmountable stumbling blocks.

After the service, a group of those in attendance met to determine what they could do together to unify our community. The outcome was to formulate a process to build a house on Brown Street in Rochester. With the Flower City Habitat for Humanity, a non-denominational Christian housing ministry helping to eliminate substandard and poverty housing in Rochester, NY, the project moved forward.

***

In February of 1999 the church added a kitchenette on the first floor of the IUCC building. Pat Partridge drew the plans from Jane Burleigh, Jane Linder and Phyllis McRae's design ideas. Larry Clarke suggested the addition of a pass-through window, and Tom Reardon and Randy McDonald headed the construction. The kitchenette was stocked with dishes, silverware, serving and cooking utensils, allowing those who held meetings on the first floor to provide refreshments without going down to the basement kitchen.

# African Children's Choir

In April of 1999 the African Children's Choir was sponsored by the Irondequoit United Church of Christ to come and perform in the church. The African Children's Choir was formed in 1984 in the midst of Uganda's bloody civil war by human rights activist Ray Barnett.

**African Childrens Choir**

Mr. Barnett was called on to help the many thousands of orphaned and starving children, abandoned and helpless to feed and protect themselves. Realizing the enormity of the task, he and his team came up with a unique approach. The only way to make a meaningful difference was to impact the lives of these children one child at a time. *"Inspired by the singing of one small boy, we formed the first African Children's Choir to show the world that Africa's most vulnerable children have beauty, dignity and unlimited ability."*

In the early years the African Children's choir principally toured in North America, Canada and Britain. The proceeds of their tours and the sponsorship support funded a growing program to established literacy schools.

No less could be expected than to have the IUCC packed with church members, and guests from all over the city of Rochester to come, hear and see the awe inspiring performance of the children. Babs Reimensnyder spearheaded the invitation to the African's Children Choir and spread the news of this upcoming event at the Irondequoit United Church of Christ.  The event met with success.

****

Now a tradition, the Bike Hike marked its twentieth year in 1999.  There were plenty of riders, plenty of fun and plenty of companionship, making the event another year of success.

The church was entering the new century with good representation to the community, the church and foreign affairs. We were an inspiring church family.

In July of 1999 the collaborative Habitat for Humanity project was underway. IUCC joined other churches in participating in building a home on Fulton Avenue. While background work was done earlier, the coalition of nine Irondequoit communities worked together over the next six months to raise money for the ambitious project  and to take part in building homes for residents.

****

In January 2000 a reception was held for the Rev. Jerry Smith, who had tendered his resignation as pastor the previous month. After five years, he planned to move on to be the pastor at the First Trinitarian Congregational Church in Scituate, Massachusetts. At his parting, the Rev. Dale Davis accepted the position of Interim Pastor.

**Saying Goodbye To Rev. Jerry Smith**

***

This was the year of the formation of the Girls' Choir by Joe Gabalski, the church's Music Director. The group was made up of girls in grades six to twelve and at its upstart there were fourteen members.

Youth also participated in the 30-Hour Famine for World Vision. World Vision's 30 Hour Famine is a worldwide movement of students who are serious about serving God and fighting hunger  and it is done on an empty stomach.  For 30 hours, students get a taste of hunger by not eating so they know what it feels like for those more than a billion people around the world who experience hunger every day.

Along with not eating the students do fundraising activities, community service projects , helping them to learn more about the facts of world hunger.  The process is easy enough with each group having to sign up to participate in the Famine.  After a group is signed up, the youth leader will receive a Welcome Kit that will have everything needed to hold a successful Famine.

In the weeks approaching the Famine event, participants raise money to help feed hungry kids and once the Famine begins, students turn in the funds they've raised so far to the group leader to send in to World Vision. At the end of the 30 hours the  group breaks the fast and many choose to start with communion.   To finish strong with Famine Sunday the participants take over the church service on Sunday and share their Famine experience with the whole congregation.  This program encourages young people everywhere to share the love of Christ with hungry children and families around the world.

## Long Time Traditions Continue

Traditions of old continued, such as the Bike Hike and the Crop Walk to support issues in the community. Just as important were becoming the yearly Chicken Barbecue and the Strawberry Festival held at the IUCC. This year would be special for the Strawberry Festival as it represented the 20th annual festival held that June in 2000. Members eagerly offered to help.

Helen Rice scoops strawberries on the shortbread

The pictures above shows Helen Rice as she scoops berries onto shortbread, outside on the lawn of IUCC, and below Joe and Katie Izzo appear beside the sign in front of the church announcing the upcoming Strawberry Festival. That year, as in the past, the outcome was successful for unity with the community, financial income for the church, and enjoying the great taste of a wonderful tradition for the community as a whole.

Continuing to use the talent in our midst, the musical "Joseph and the Amazing Technicolor Dreamcoat" was presented in three performances at IUCC. The cast included thirty children, and another thirty participants were part of the children's choir.

The initiative of church members lead to continuous outreach, such as Back Bay Mission (BBM). Helen Rice served as planner, director and prime worker in the support of this worthwhile program. IUCC Women's Fellowship has traditionally donated to them and in 1992, 1994 and 1996 they received a portion of the St. Paul Legacy to Humanity Fund. The BBM staff members travel to different sections of the country to put on Shrimp Boil Dinners at sponsoring churches on successive nights. In May of 2000 they were hosted at IUCC.

# Rev. Dale Davis (2000-2008)

Dale & Mrs. Davis
Hannah & Cameron Davis

***

In 2001 the Irondequoit United Church of Christ welcomed its new pastor, the Rev. Dale Davis, in a traditional installation ceremony followed by a celebration meal prepared in the dining room. Pastor Dale helped take the church into the 21st century after coming and serving as the interim minister in 2000.

**Rev. Dale Davis Is Installed As The New Minister**

OUR STAFF

Bottom Row: Pastor Sarah Greenfield Culp, Pastor Emeritus Dr. Robert Bermudes, Senior Pastor Dale Davis. Middle Row: Sexton Robert Karvetski, Office Administrator Carol Confer. Top Row: Music Director Colleen Curry and Business Operations Manager Larry Clarke.

**Welcoming Rev. Davis**

# Christ on the Mount Painting

In 2001 the church was visited by a film crew, a producer and director from Hollywood, a local cinematographer, and a photographer, Chris Hart. The object was the filming of a documentary on the work and life of Batiste Madalena, the artist who painted "Christ on the Mount" on the chancel wall in the sanctuary.

Batiste Madalena working on our *SERMON ON THE MOUNT* in his studio in Downtown Rochester

In the early 1920s, George Eastman, founder of Eastman Kodak, decided to build a showcase theater in Rochester, his hometown. He built the Eastman Theater, at the time the third largest cinema in the U.S. and one of the most elaborate. He commissioned a local artist, Batiste Madalena, to create all his movie posters. From 1924 until 1928, working alone over a four-year period and against deadlines that required as many as eight new posters a week for each change of bill, Madalena created over 1,400 unique works, and to our credit we have one as the background to our sanctuary.

Director Mel Powell and Producer Lori Bertheisen met with the historian, Ann Smith, on June 29 to film an interview about IUCC and the history of the painting

Also in 2001, the IUCC senior high youth group put on a Shrove Tuesday Pancake Supper. Shrove Tuesday is the term used in Ireland, the United Kingdom Australia, Canada, and among U.S. Episcopalians to refer to the day after Shrove Monday (or the more old fashioned Collop Monday) and before Ash Wednesday, when the Christian liturgical season of Lent begins.

Among other activities that year, the congregation approved a capital fund drive to pay for needed repairs requiring approximately $255,000. The high school youth participated in the annual 30-Hour Fast, and the Strawberry Festival and Chicken Barbecue continued to attract more people.

"The Lighted Cross" newsletter continued, with additions to the standard church news. This year they added a Family News section that gave details on members. This was a way of getting to know our neighbors personally.

***

Ruth Circle, a long-standing church circle that meets monthly, celebrated Helen Rice's ninetieth birthday with a dinner. In the picture are Pearl Hess, Doc Kendall, Helen Rice and Eunice Osborne.

To show how much Helen is appreciated, a song and poem were written for her. Helen has been an active member of the church for many years.

***

Our Congregation in 2000 filled the church as it had in the pass.  It was a time of prosper for not only IUCC, but the community at large.

This proved to be a big year for the IUCC Girl's Choir, which traveled to Italy for a concert to tighten bonds with our town's sister city, Pescara, Italy.

The Bike Hike in 2001 proved to be a real challenge. That year the mercury already read in the low 80s at 8:00 a.m., but as happened over the years, the camaraderie was strong.

The group started with prayer for the three-day event that would have them arriving back at the church on Sunday afternoon. Each year the group has continued to have old and some new members join them. They camp socialize and play games, making this a wonderful adventure for the riders .

## Event of September 11, 2001

The events of September 11, 2001 were a series of coordinated suicide attacks by al-Qaeda upon the United States. That morning, nineteen Islamic terrorists hijacked four commercial passenger jet airliners. The hijackers intentionally crashed two of the airliners into the Twin Towers of the World Trade Center in New York City, killing everyone on board and many others working in the building. Both buildings collapsed within two hours, destroying at least two nearby buildings and damaging others. The hijackers crashed a third airliner into the Pentagon. The fourth plane crashed into a field near Shanksville in rural Somerset County, Pennsylvania, after some of its passengers and flight crew attempted to retake control of the plane, which the hijackers had redirected toward Washington, D.C. There were no survivors from any of the flights.

The service held at IUCC to respond to the terrorism shows the sentiment expressed for the loss of life and family sorrow.

Always feeling for others, the congregation came to pray for those families who had suffered a loss with song and spiritual blessings.

During the service, the Sankofa Dance and Drum Ensemble performed to the music of an eclectic mix of drum, dance and songs. Sankofa is led by Kofi, an Asante prince from Ghana , and Yacin, a Wollof princess from Senegal . The group consists of dancers, and singers and two drummers. Formed in 1997, the group teaches togetherness in diversity and the empowerment of the individual self-image, as well as community building through African drumming and dance.

Those who attended the service came away with hope for the future of the country, those who had suffered a loss, and felt the unity as each one prayed for peace.

In October of 2001, the Rev. Robert W. Bermudes became Pastor Emeritus of IUCC.  He had previously served as the IUCC minister from 1972 until 1993 and the reconnection was well received.

Rev. Bermudes quoted a philosopher who once wrote that "We cannot know where we are to go until we examine where we have been." Following the installation, a luncheon was held in his honor. Rev. Bermudes shared with us that he was extremely pleased that our pastor, Dale Davis, and repeatedly said the time is right for the Irondequoit United Church Of Christ to connect the past with the present so that everyone may have a clearer vision of the future. He saw this honor as being a part of our future.

## Salem Soup Kitchen

Each Monday and Tuesday from noon to 1 p.m., several hundred of Rochester's neediest citizens gather in Salem United Church of Christ's Gymnasium for a warm meal and an experience of respectful community.  Each Monday that they are open, an 11:00 a.m. Bible study is also offered, with clothing distributed once a month. Volunteers from over forty different churches and other organizations offer their time and love to serve guests, and many IUCC members have volunteered here over the years.

Members of our congregation, such as Lois Metzger, pictured here, not only prepare and serve food, but members of Ruth Circle also

prepare and bring eggs and brownies to our church on designated
Sundays to be served at the Salem Soup Kitchen.

## The National Register of Historic Places

In 2001 the Board of Trustees engaged Ann Parks to prepare
the application for the church building to be listed as a historic place.
Rick Zuegel was chosen to submit the necessary photos. Registry as a
historic building could affect the capital campaign, in that the building
might become eligible for grants were it officially designated.  Dick
Ahlman, Chairman of the Board of Trustees, introduced Cynthia Howk,
Research Coordinator on the staff of the Landmark Society of Western
New York, who informed the board that IUCC could be the first
building in the town of Irondequoit to be designated a historic place.
She stressed that there would be no restrictions on future changes or
improvements were it to be placed on the official registry.

A special Thank You went out to Mrs. Ruth Hecker and her late husband, John C. Hecker for graciously offering to underwrite the expense of hiring a consultant to help IUCC apply for a listing on The National Register of Historic Places.

This was the beginning of the process that would be revisited.

HECKER, Ruth

***

On January 6, 2002 IUCC welcomed new refugees known as the Lost Boys of Sudan, who were among the more than 27,000 boys who were displaced and/or orphaned during the Second Sudanese Civil War that began in 1983.

Many of the boys came from the predominantly Christian southern section of Sudan and fled persecution by Muslims, who dominated northern Sudan.

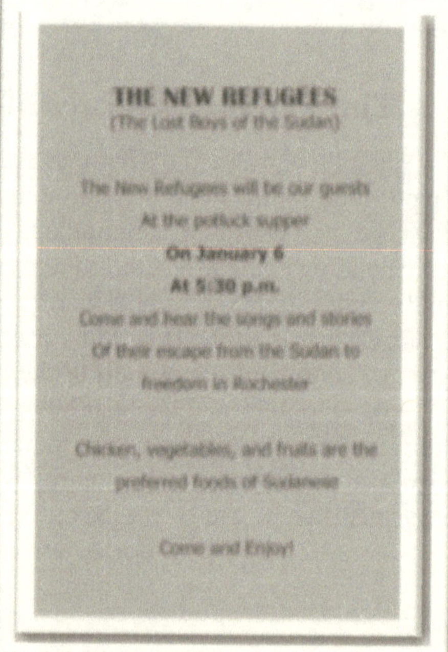

This name was given by aid organizations, including the International Rescue Committee, when in 2001 about 3800 Lost Boys arrived in the United States, where they are now scattered in about thirty-eight cities, averaging one hundred per city.

In February 2002 Colleen Curry, who had served as Director of Music, resigned, and Bruce and Kathy Beardsley returned to assume positions as Interim Director of Music and Organist.

Long missed, the Beardsley easily fit into the role that they had previously held and for some it felt like old times.  For those who were new to the church, it was easy to recognized the importance of the Beardsley to our church.

*** 

A controversy that prevailed in the congregation was the removal of the flags from the sanctuary. Pros and cons were presented, but after 9/11 the issue became more heated. After a series of meetings and discussions, the flags were reintroduced to the sanctuary on Boy Scout Sunday, in February 2002. The ceremony, entitled

"*Reintroduction of Flags into the Sanctuary*," was heartwarming. The prayer of introduction follows:

We welcome these flags into the sanctuary, not as symbols to be worshiped, O Lord, but as a reminder of the role that you have played in the past, present and future of our country.

We place them in this sanctuary acknowledging that you, O God, are the Supreme Being.

*Let them stand as a visible means of our prayers for your blessing upon us. Let their presence be an acknowledgement that all we do, as a nation, should be done in your service, in your spirit, and in keeping with your will. Keep us mindful, through their presence, that all the prosperity and security we enjoy as a nation is due to your bountiful gift, and your grace. Amen.*

## Historical Landmark Acceptance

In 2002 the Landmark Society of Western New York presented the Irondequoit United Church of Christ for National Register nomination. The Landmark Society of Western New York, Inc., was organized in 1937 and is one of the oldest and most active preservation organizations in America. Their mission is to discover, protect, and revitalize the architectural and related cultural heritage of the Rochester region, and to educate and inform the community about that heritage.

The request then went to the State Historic Preservation Office (SHPO), which helps communities identify, evaluate, preserve and revitalize historic, archeological and cultural resources. The SHPO administers programs authorized by both the National Historic Preservation Act of 1966 and the New York State Historic Preservation Act of 1980. After a long and stressful process, IUCC was recognized. In the finalized document, the church is described in such detail that it is as good as a picture.

**United States Department of the Interior**
**National Park Service**
**NATIONAL REGISTER OF HISTORIC**
**PLACES**
**OMS No. 1024-0018, NPS Form**
**United Congregational Church of Irondequoit**
**Monroe County, New York**

The United Congregational Church of Irondequoit is located on a 1.7-acre parcel on the north side of Titus Avenue, and at the northeast corner of Ganado Street in the town of Irondequoit. Titus Avenue is one of the principal east-west streets in the town. The surrounding neighborhood is composed of early-to-late-20th century residences and commercial buildings.

The complex is comprised of three interconnected buildings, which together form a large square with a narrow open courtyard at the center. The rectangular Colonial Revival style church is oriented on a north-south axis on the west side of the parcel. A one-story hyphen on the east side of the church connects the church building, along the front facade, to the Arts & Crafts style brick Women's Christian Temperance Union (WCTU) building. The WCTU building, originally a cross shape, is attached at the north end to a plain, brick Colonial Revival style Sunday School building. Together, the WCTU and Sunday school have a rectangular footprint of equal length to the church. The church building is linked to the Sunday School building by a one-story hyphen at the rear.

The church is constructed of variegated tan and reddish-colored brick laid in common bond with trim of buff colored Norristone (a brand of cast stone) and wood. Cast-stone elements include the foundation and entrance steps, window hoodmoulds, keystones, sills, and quoins. Wood elements include window and door surrounds, decorative cornice detail, belfry and lantern tower, and the pedimented entrance porch. The low-pitched gable roofs of the nave and entrance porch are sheathed with asphalt.

The principal (south) facade is dominated by a central three-stage engaged tower above a two-story, three-bay pedimented entrance portico. The pediment is ornamented with simple bracketed molding on the cornice and a multi-paned oculus window centered in the pediment. The portico roofline is lower than the roofline of the nave, so that the cornice line above the simple entablature, which supports the pediment, connects and duplicates the bracketed molded cornice of the nave. Supporting the pediment are four fluted columns across the front and two pilasters in the rear; all with Roman Ionic capitals. The portico rests on an elevated cast-stone foundation and porch with six steps and wrought-iron railings on three sides.

The principal entrance is located in the base of the tower and is composed of double four-panel doors with a round-arched, multi-paned fanlight in a keystoned, round-arched surround, which in turn is surrounded by a simple pediment supported a narrow, plain entablature above slender half-rounded columns with Roman Ionic capitals. Flanking the entrance and tower are round-arched, multi-light sash windows with cast-stone lintels and hoodmoulds. Above the entrance and each round-arched window is a multi-light sash window topped by a simple cast-stone keystone. On either side of the portico, on the first floor, is a narrow, 6-light single-sash window, also topped by a stone keystone.

The engaged brick base of the tower rises above the pedimented nave, both of which are accented by cast-stone quoins and simple, bracketed mouldings on the wood cornices. The belfry stage of the tower is wood; each of the four faces features a flat pedestal base. above which are round-arched louvered openings in keystone surrounds. with the louvers in the arch arranged like a fan. The belfry comers are embellished with Roman Ionic pilasters. Above the simple entablature and cornice of the belfry rests a balustrade topped by an urn finial on each comer post. The lantern stage above is octagonal with round-arched multi-sash windows on each face, ending with a simple entablature, A plain cross has been applied onto the front face. The hexagonal copper dome roof terminates in a simple metal weathervane.

The west facade is divided longitudinally into six principal bays. The first bay, closest to the front facade, contains an oculus window with divided lights embellished with four stone keystones. Under the window, there is an attached, one-story, enclosed brick entrance porch with a cast-stone foundation and six cast-stone steps with wrought-iron railings leading to the recessed double entrance doors of divided lights. The classical door surround is composed of narrow Doric pilasters supporting a simple wide entablature and a molded cornice. Each of the north and south facades of the entrance porch is similarly adorned with narrow Doric pilasters supporting a simple wide entablature. The entrance porch has a flat roof. The next four bays consist of large round-arched windows with a sub-arched portion that incorporates the 32-over-16 double-hung sash windows. Within the principal arch and flanking the double-hung windows are 16-over-8 double-hung sash sidelights. The sub-arch and its extensions of the window are comprised of plain, wide painted wood. The fanlight portions of the principal and sub-arch are glazed in sunburst lights pattern and convex arches attached to the intrados, matching those on the principal facade. The entire window is embellished by a cast-stone hoodmould with a key-console. The sixth bay is composed of an oculus window matching the first bay and a round-arched single entrance doorway. The door is paneled on the lower half with 12 divided lights on the upper half; above the door is a round-arched, divided fan light matching the windows.

The east facade of the church duplicates the west facade, except that at either end of the facade the two one-story hyphens connect the church building to the WCTU building (at the front) and the Sunday School (at the rear).

A cast-stone watertable marks the top of the smooth, random ashlar cast-stone foundation. Below each window bay is a pair of 8-over-8 double-hung basement windows with shallow window wells.

At the rear of the principal church building is a smaller, one-story portion with paired, 12-over-12 double-hung windows on the west and east facades, and two bays of paired 12-over-12 double-hung windows on the north facade: below each are paired 8-over-8 double-hung windows embedded into the cast-stone foundation and raised so that the watertable wraps around the upper portion of the windows. A narrow rectangular louvered vent with keystone and cast-stone sill is located at the gable end of the one-story portion; an oculus window, matching the others, is located in the gable end of the principal church building.

The main entrance doors on the front facade open into a small vestibule in the base of the tower. The vestibule in turn leads into the narthex. through a pair of entrance doors with divided light windows and a divided-light transom. The narthex spans the width of the nave beneath a balcony with three sections of tiered pews. Two staircases with turned balusters lead to the nave balcony. The narthex is separated from the nave by multi-paned glazed screen accented with pilasters: glazed double center doors provide access to the nave. The front of the balcony is adorned with plain, recessed rectangular panels, above which are four, Doric columns, which support a simple entablature that connects to the main entablature on both sides of the nave. The tower mass at the center of the balcony's back wall is broken by a recessed, elliptical arch. Centered on the wall above the balcony entablature is a semi-circular open louvered fan with keystone, behind which was to be an echo organ.

Each of the two side aisles is separated from the center of the nave by three Doric columns on hexagonal plinths that support a simple entablature, which, in turn, is also supported at the chancel end by a Doric pilaster.

Evenly spaced between each window is a simple, wood Doric pilaster, with its base and plinth matching the height of the columns. A plain chair rail connects to the base of the window. Beneath each window is a boxed heating element, which consists of a wood 3-panel frame, the lower portions with open metal grate, the upper closed metal grates. The slightly projecting frame is topped by stained wood sill. The divided-light windows consist of

plain opaque and pastel-colored glass in a random pattern.
The molded window surround is topped by a keystone
that is incorporated into a simple, narrow entablature that
runs just below the ceiling and above the pilasters.

At the end of each side aisle flanking the chancel,
is a six-paneled door, above which are a small
pedimented, hymnal panel and a divided-light false
window topped with a broken pediment with a center urn
relief. Centered in the upper three rows of each of the
window's divided lights is a convex-curved diamond
mullion within an oval mullion. These windows hide the
organ pipes, along with three round-arched, divided-light
windows that face each side of the chancel. Separating
each side window is a simple Doric pilaster. Above these
windows, and continuing around the chancel is the same
wide entablature which continues from the nave into the
chancel and ends at the center panel of the chancel wall.
Within the entablature, above each window is an open
screen, composed of thin vertical slats; in between each is
a vertical, louvered ellipse. The lower portion of the
chancel walls has wood paneling, consisting of a tall
vertical panel, topped by a small horizontal panel.

The end wall of the chancel is dominated by
large painted mural, "Christ on the Mount," by Batiste
Madalena, which is divided into five panels. The panels
are separated by wooden pilasters, which support the
entablature:

Above the center portion is a semi-circular
louvered fan with keystone, similar to the one at the south
end of the nave above the balcony. The painting depicts
Christ standing on a rocky promontory against a clouded
sky.

The pews in the nave and chancel furniture,
which includes the three-panel pulpit with rounded
pilasters, the organ console enclosure, boxed choir stalls,
small lectern, are composed of paneled wood that
matches the paneling on the walls of the chancel. All
surfaces of the church interior are painted white, except
for the chancel doors, the pew seats and backs, and the
top railings of the side panels of the pews, choir stalls and
furniture, which are dark-stained wood. The barrel-
vaulted nave ceiling is painted blue. Lighting for the nave
and chancel is provided by hexagonal glass and wrought-
iron lantern-style fixtures, which hang by long chains

from the ceiling; each of the nave fixtures has an additional ring of electric candles at the base of the lantern.

A painted door at either end of the north chancel wall leads to a large room, located in the one-story addition attached to the principal church building, which originally served as the "ladies parlor" and currently is used by the choir. On the chancel wall is a fireplace surrounded by painted white wood paneling. The room is lit by paired double-hung windows.

The dark-stained six-panel doors at the north end of the side aisles lead to staircases that proceed to the basement level where the original kitchen and open dining hall are located.

East of the church building is the Women's Christian Temperance Union building (WCTU), which is attached to the church by a one-story, brick, four-bay hyphen, slightly recessed from the front facade of the church. The foundation of the link matches that of the main church structure. The cornice is simple and the roof is gabled and covered with asphalt. The identical bays feature full-story, round-arched windows with paired divided-light panels and round-arched detailing matching that of the church. The north side of the link consists of one round-arched, divided-light window and a round-arched, divided-light door matching those on the front; the door leads to an outside, narrow flag-stoned and landscaped Memorial Garden courtyard, situated in the open space between the two buildings.

The WCTU building is a two-story building constructed of brick, its facade color matching that of the church, with cast-stone quoins. Originally standing by itself in the shape of a cross, its exterior form is now t-shaped, with its rear connecting directly to the current Sunday School building. The asphalt roof is cross-hipped with a flat top. The front facade is divided into three bays. The center bay contains the elevated main entrance, with a simple porch entry and eight stone steps with a plain iron railing. The porch pediment is embellished with simple brackets that match those on the church portico, and is supported by plain square columns with simple bases, but without capitals or entablature, and plain pilasters. The entrance surround is unembellished. The double doors are wood-paneled on the lower half and glazed on the upper half. Above the entrance are three round-arched, double-hung windows with divided lights and with simple, brick hoodmoulds. The two bays flanking the entrance consist of a single round-arched window, matching the size and description of those in the center bay, located at the second floor level, but lower than the windows in the center bay. Also included are basement windows with divided lights. Centered in the roof slope is a single dormer with a deck roof and six-over-six double-hung window; the sides of the dormer is sheathed with wood clapboard siding.

The east elevation is divided into the two sections of the exposed cross plan. The facade closest to the front contains two bays: one round-arched double-hung window matching the size, height and location of those on the front facade; the second bay consisting of a pair of six-aver-six, double-hung windows, one each on the first and second floors. The projecting facade has a two-story, round-arched window on the short south elevation, cast-stone quoins on the comers, and, on the east elevation, a set of four two-story, round-arched, 12-over-12 double-hung windows-the arched portion above the double-hung sections matches that of the other windows. At the basement level, there are three-aver-three double-hung windows under each main window.

The interior retains its original basic layout: a central, rectangular, two-story hall with rooms opening off around it. Originally open through both stories with a balcony and walkway with glass doors on the second-story rooms, the central hall has been closed to the second floor with walls and a hipped ceiling. The interior contains administrative offices and meeting spaces and has no significant detailing.

The two-story, brick Sunday School addition attaches to the rear of the WCTU building, wrapping around the cross end of the former building to retain a flush facade for two bays, continuing with a projecting entrance facade with a two-story portico, and ending with a three bay section, The addition is nearly square, and. combined with \VCTU, is rectangular matching the length of the main church building. The brick is more reddish in color than that of the WCTU and church buildings. Cast-stone trim is limited to the window sills, a belt course between the first and second floor. and a plain narrow frieze just below the roof line, The roof is flat and covered with asphalt. Windows are simple 8-over-8 double hung. A plain, one-story link, with an entrance, connects to the rear portion of the church building. The all-wood entrance portico is pedimented with a triangular insert, beneath which is a molded entablature supported by four slender Doric columns. The entrance door is also pedimented, matching the portico in detailing; the double doors, all glazed with divided lights, are flanked by Doric pilasters. Two concrete steps and a concrete ramp lead to the entrance.

The main church building maintains a high degree of integrity on both the interior and exterior. The WCTU building has been altered on the exterior from its original all-Arts & Crafts appearance by the replacement of

the original Arts & Crafts entrance porch and dormer with a Colonial Revival entry and dormer to harmonize with the church building. In addition, the building facade was re-clad with new brick and cast-stone 'quoins to match those of the church building. The interior also has been greatly altered to serve as administrative functions. Except for the brick color, the restrained, utilitarian design of the Sunday School building blends, but remains secondary to the two earlier structures.

The parcel includes a long, narrow asphalt parking lot on the east side and a smaller, square parking lot on the north side that is separated from the structures by a grass lawn. On the west side of the church are evergreen shrubs planted between the basement window bays, a narrow strip of grass, and a sidewalk with several mature trees along Ganado Street. The front and east sides of the WCTU building are also landscaped with foundation shrubs and a small lawn area with an ornamental tree on the east side.

The United Congregational Church of Irondequoit is architecturally significant as an outstanding, intact example of a Colonial Revival style church in the town of Irondequoit. Designed in 1926 by the Rochester architectural firm of Foote and Carpenter, the United Congregational Church of Irondequoit exhibits a high degree of sophistication in its interpretation of the late eighteenth and early nineteenth century New England meeting house models and features exceptional neoclassical detailing on both the exterior and interior. As the largest and most sophisticated ecclesiastical building in the town of Irondequoit when it was built, the church also reflects the town's rapid change during the 1920s from a farming community to a growing residential suburb of Rochester.

The name "Irondequoit" originates from the Seneca Indians, and generally means "where the land and waters meet." The town is bounded by Lake Ontario on the north, the Genesee River on the west, Irondequoit Bay on the east, and the city of Rochester on the south. Before the area was permanently settled in the early nineteenth century, the Senecas, and later the French and English used the upper Genesee River, the Irondequoit Bay, and foot trails in between, including the elevated east-west Ridge Road, as transportation routes. The Indian Landing at the foot of Irondequoit Bay served as an important trading center for the Senecas. The two villages established in the town were short-lived and were initially planned as trading centers with links to Canada. The City of Tryon, founded in 1799 at the Indian Landing, was eventually deserted about 1820 when ships could no longer navigate the bay because of sandbars. The village of Carthage, established on the banks of the Upper Genesee River in the first decade of the nineteenth century, flourished until the Erie Canal opened in 1825 and the booming village of Rochesterville became the principal commercial center. When the city of Rochester was incorporated in 1834, Carthage became part of the city. Indeed, from 1840 until 1923, the city continued to annex southern portions of the town.

When the town of Irondequoit was incorporated in 1839, hunting and fishing were still the principal activities in the area as three-quarters of the land was still an unsettled wilderness with swamps, gullies, rocky soils, and dense forests. Much of the timber used for construction in the boomtown of Rochester in this period came from Irondequoit. As trees were cleared from the land, farmers began raising crops. By 1830, most of the major north-south and east-west arteries, including Titus Avenue, were laid out. As early as 1835 and well into the early twentieth century, Irondequoit became known for its small, but intensively worked fruit and vegetable farms. Peaches and melons were among the major crops.

Between 1880 and 1920, the nursery business was a leading industry in the town with Rochester serving as the center of trade. One of the first nurserymen was George Cooper whose farm was located at the comer of Cooper Road and Titus A venue. He later entered the vegetable gardening business.

Throughout the nineteenth century and into the first two decades of the twentieth century there was little population growth within the town limits. As population grew in the southern part of the town, these areas were annexed by the City of Rochester in six annexations. Farming remained as the principal activity in the remaining part of the town. While electric streetcar and interurban railroad lines were built on the far eastern and western edges of the town. the resident population of the town remained under 5.000 until 1920. These transit lines brought city residents to the summer resort and recreation areas on the shores of Lake Ontario and Irondequoit Bay around the turn of the century and spurred limited residential development immediately adjacent to their routes. With the advent of the automobile, the town began its m,-~or and rapid transformation from a farming and recreational community to a residential suburb of Rochester. Between 1920 and 1925, the population doubled, from 5,123 to 10,469. The Plat maps of 1904, 1924, and 1935 dramatically show the rapid change and development in Irondequoit, particularly around Titus Avenue and Cooper Road, where farms gave way to residential subdivisions on the n0l1h side of Titus Avenue and commercial development on the south side. The 1910 former Grange Hall, located on the south of Titus A venue opposite the church, remains as the sole reminder of the area's farming heritage.

The United Congregational Church of Irondequoit grew out of the Irondequoit Union Sabbath School, which was established by a small group of devoted women in 1850. It was the first religious organization in the town. Irondequoit residents usually drove to Rochester to attend churches, but there was a growing desire for more religious opportunity near home. The Sunday School met in the small District 3 schoolhouse, located on the southeast comer of Titus A venue and Cooper Road. Teachers and pastors from Rochester churches of several denominations came to teach at the school in the morning and, beginning in 1853, preach services in the afternoons. During the period of religious revivals in 1850s and the 1870s, Sunday evening preaching services were added. However, most Irondequoit residents continued to travel into Rochester for morning worship. Among those presenting sermons at the services were students from the Rochester Theological Seminary (now Colgate Rochester Divinity School). In 1861 the schoolhouse was demolished and a two-room brick school was erected on the opposite, northwest, comer of Titus Avenue and Cooper Road.

In 1880, seven women from the community, some active in the Sunday School, organized a local branch of the 'Women's Christian Temperance Union and began meeting in the District 3 schoolhouse. In 1885, a frame hall was built just west of the school on Titus A venue and was officially dedicated to religious and temperance work. Soon the W.C.T.U. invited the Sunday School to hold its classes in the new building, and a thirty-year· collaboration began with the two groups. In 1891, the W.C.T.U. hall was enlarged to accommodate an expanding Sunday School. Both groups worked closely together in fund-raising events to support their separate and combined interests, while remaining distinct and independent organizations. On October 28, 1901, a fire destroyed the Hall and its entire contents. Funds were soon raised by both organizations to construct a new building, and before the end of 1910, Sunday School classes began meeting in the basement of the new brick building (the present W.C.T.U. building), which was completed and dedicated in January 1911.

When the idea of forming a church was first conceived, early in 1911, no organized church existed in the town of Irondequoit. Many families still preferred to retain their memberships in Rochester churches. Homes were canvassed by a Sunday School committee, however, and the Congregation denomination was chosen because its liberal government seemed to offer an acceptable common ground for the several churches represented in the organizing body. On February 9, 1911 the first meeting of the United Congregational Church of Irondequoit was held with 204 charter members, of which 118 by transfer of letter from six other churches. On November 8, 1911 the W.C.T.U. voted to deed its land

and new Hall to the United Congregational Church. At the same time the Union Sabbath School approved the transfer and changed its name to the Sabbath School of United Congregational Church.

Years of growth followed and. in the fall of 1919, the congregation voted to raise funds for the purchase the lot on Titus Avenue, adjacent to and west of the W.C.T.U. Building, and the eventual erection of a church building. In May 1926, the comer stone of the present church was laid, and the first service in the new building was held on Christmas Sunday, December 26, 1926. At the official dedication ceremonies on February 27, 1927, the original (W.C.T.U.) building became the Sunday School.

According to a newspaper article of November _, 1926, "Members of this church believe that they have the only edifice of Georgian Colonial architecture in the vicinity of Rochester."  The congregation hired the firm of Foote and Carpenter to design its new edifice. Although the firm existed in a formal way only between 1922 to 1928, the two architects had worked together since 1914.  Orlando Foote (1854-1930) is best known for his design of the notable neo-Romanesque Third Presbyterian Church (1893, National Register listed as a contributing component of the East A venue Historic District, 1979), at the comer of East Avenue and Meigs Street in Rochester.  Charles Carpenter (1885-1952) was associated with numerous churches, schools, and public buildings in Rochester, as well as in New York State.

There may be several reasons why the congregation (or perhaps, the architect) selected this style of architecture. The Georgian/Colonial Revival style was at its peak of popularity for both residential and institutional construction during this period. The neoclassical Wren-Gibbs formula for church design is also strongly associated with New England, the traditional stronghold of Congregationalism in America. This tradition came to western New York in the very late eighteenth and early nineteenth centuries with the waves of settlers moving west from largely Calvinist (i.e. Congregationalist and Presbyterian) New England. Architects of the period were familiar with the Georgian and Adam prototypes from such publications as the 1915 White Pine Series of Architectural Monographs, which contained photographs of colonial buildings, including several early New England meeting houses. Before he came to Rochester around 1880, architect Orlando K. Foote first worked in the offices of the nationally renowned Boston firm of McKim, Mead & White, and may have traveled with the architects during their widely publicized tour of New England in 1877. Foote's only known major ecclesiastical work was the Third Presbyterian Church in Rochester, which was designed in the neo-Romanesque style in 1893. Indeed, most of the churches in the area that were built in the late nineteenth and early twentieth century were designed in the Gothic Revival style. The Irondequoit United Church of Christ is the only major Colonial Revival style religious building in the Rochester region.

After the American Revolution, the Puritan meeting house form evolved into a church plan and style that was inspired by English architect Christopher Wren and his protégé, James Gibbs, developed in their rebuilding of central London after the Great Fire of 1666. The Wren-Gibbs prototype, exemplified by churches such as St. Martin's-in-the-Fields, feature an engaged tower at the center of the facade, neoclassical detailing, and often include a colonnaded portico across the facade. The towers of these churches are surmounted by tiered bell towers that use the neoclassical decorative vocabulary while evoking the vertical silhouette of a Gothic spire. Initially employed in America by Anglican churches, the style was adopted by most Protestant denominations during the course of the eighteenth century, albeit with interior arrangements more suited to their particular needs.

The builders' guides of Asher Benjamin (1771-1845) provided a means by which country builders could plan and construct meeting houses in the style popularized by Charles Bulfinch. His "Plans of Meetinghouse and Pulpit" in The Country Builder's Assistant (1797) were copied and adapted in hundreds of edifices throughout New England. Indeed, the Irondequoit United Church of Christ can be compared with several New England edifices with colonnaded porticos, among which are the Congregational churches in Windsor. Vermont, and in Litchfield, Cheshire, and Guilford, Connecticut

The architecture of the United Congregational Church of Irondequoit reflects the traditional model of the neoclassical style New England meeting house of the Federal period in its overall form. The building also evokes the sophisticated city churches of such centers as London and Boston in its use of brick; (cast) stone trim and finely wrought neoclassical detailing. The building's interior also hearkens back to the Wren-Gibbs tradition in the use of a prominent altar/table with flanking choir stalls, lectern and pulpit rather than a prominent central pulpit, and in its use of pale painted woodwork accented by very dark Finished wood trim.

The applied cross on the front face of the octagonal lantern stage of the Irondequoit church tower was added during World War II. Normally, Congregational churches did not display a cross on their steeples; however, the Bausch & Lomb company, located in Rochester on St. Paul Street, approached the congregation about adding a lighted cross because the church steeple was the necessary height and distance from their company plant to test the calibration of their Norden Bomb Sight.

At the end of World War II, an Honor Roll Committee was established to create a memorial for two church members who gave their lives in military service during the war. The result was a mural entitled "Christ on the Mount," painted by local artist Batiste Madalena in the blind Palladian arcade at the back of the chancel. The mural was dedicated October 15, 1950 in memory of the two soldiers and to recognize others from the church who served their country in World Wars I and II.

Batiste Madalena (1902-1988) was a Rochester artist who executed hand-painted movie posters during the "Golden Era of the Silent Screen," Hired by George Eastman as the Eastman Theatre's artist-in-residence, Madalena created 1,400 original poster paintings, an average of eight per week. One-hundred-two of his works are now in the collection of the Academy of Motion Pictures Arts and Sciences in Beverly Hills, California, while others are housed at the Smithsonian Institution and the Museum of Modern Art. He later executed portraits and window displays for local department stores. The church painting is believed to be Madalena's only religious artwork.

In 1951, an addition was built onto the W.C.T.U. building to expand the Sunday School. In 1957, the church became a congregation of the United Church of Christ, a new denomination resulting from the merger of the Congregational Church and the Evangelical and Reformed Church.

The church's imposing architectural presence may have influenced the style of the Irondequoit Town Hall, which is located east of the church at 1280 Titus Avenue and was built in 1951 in the Colonial Revival style. Without a village center, the town had no permanent place for government activities. Through its history the town conducted official business in various buildings until Supervisor Thomas E. Broderick, supervisor from 1928 to 1949, envisioned a permanent home for town government in the late 1920s and quietly began setting aside funds for its eventual construction on Titus Avenue. The town hall's architect, George L. Lorenz, may have been instructed to design a building to match the dignity of its ecclesiastical neighbor; the brick building's central tower and colonnaded portico bear a striking resemblance to those of the United Congregational Church of Irondequoit.

The United Congregational Church of Irondequoit remains the most prominent religious building in the town of Irondequoit and a distinguished example of its type.

The boundary of the nominated property conforms to the historic and current boundary of the nominated property as indicated by the heavy black line on the attached copy of a portion of the Town of Irondequoit tax map.

* * *

The following series of pictures show the church as it is in 2010

# The Sanctuary

**Long Angle View of Sanctuary**

**Side
Windows of
Sanctuary**

The Steeple w/Lighted Cross

East Side
Parking Lot
View

West Side View

Front View Inclusive of West Side

Front View Inclusive of West Side

Front Titus Avenue View

The Irondequoit United Church of Christ church building was officially listed as a State and National Historical Preservation Site; State acceptance became official in March 2002 and National acceptance that August. A letter from the New York State Office of Parks, Recreation and Historic Preservation dated August 20, 2002 stated that the church property had been listed on the National Register of Historic Places. The letter explained, "*Listing on the National Register recognizes the importance of these properties to the history of our country and provides them with a measure of protection.*"

The celebration of IUCC's National Historic Register status was held in November of 2002 with a special play about those who had played an important part in the church, such as Mrs. Silas Briggs, Mr. George Rudman, Ms. Susan B. Anthony, Rueben Dake and Seymour Titus.

On November 24, 2002 a dedication service was held for the placing of the historic marker on the front lawn of the church.

Following the service, the sign dedication took place. Among those present for the unveiling of the new historic designation plaque in front of the church were, from left, Dick Ahlman, Chairman of the IUCC Board of Trustees; Town Historian, Patricia Wayne; Former Deputy Director of the Landmark Society, Ann Parks; IUCC Historian, Ann Smith; church member and project benefactor Ruth Hecker; IUCC Senior Pastor, the Rev. Dale Davis; Town Supervisor, David Schantz; Church Moderator, Jim Hinman; and IUCC Associate Minister, the Rev. Sara Greenfield Culp.

At the end of 2002 the church offered thanks to Ruth Hecker for underwriting the cost of the historic marker that was placed on the front lawn of the church,

***

By this time IUCC was becoming quite professional offering plays. In March 2002 IUCC presented "*Annie*," marking the fourth consecutive year of presenting a production. The cast included sixty-four children and adults. The flyers, the programs, actors and sets were excellent, and everyone who attended any of the three days of performances was impressed.

IUCC continued its sponsorship of Sunset House hospice and raised money through the first of many Sunset House 5K Run and Fitness Walks on May 25, 2002.

## The Memorial Flag

It was a sad day when the Memorial Flag representing those in the church who had served their country, was removed and placed in storage.  The flag was removed to protect it from the elements, but no more.  A committee was created to seek funds to clean and frame the World War II flag. At the end of 2002 the church offered thanks to Marjorie and Richard Tharp for underwriting the cost of framing the WWII flag and to Ann and George Smith for purchasing the bronze plaque hung next to the flag describing its history.

Members were pleased when the memorial flag reappeared. The 32" by 48" flag with the ninety-three blue stars honored members of the congregation who had served in the war, and the two gold stars honored Robert Killup and Raymond Pitts, who gave their lives in service. The flag of 95 stars now had a place in the church again.

***

This was also the year for other changes when in April the Church Council spent half a day with members of the church's Vision

Team to engage in a time of dialogue and discovery. In October of 2001 the Church Council authorized the formation of a Vision Team whose charge was to develop a process that would ensure adequate focus on the church's future.  It was the responsibility of the VISION TEAM to ensure the success of Worship and Small Communities by building consensus with the congregation for our Vision, Core values, Mission Priorities, and Long Range Goals. The team worked with, and received support from the staff as necessary.

The Vision Teams aim is to have five (5) elected members with overlapping two-year terms. The Primary Responsibilities of the team are to:

*Continuously review, articulate, and facilitate the
process for updating the vision, core values,
mission priorities, and long-range goals of our
congregation.
Identify the needs of our community through
efforts such as public benchmarks and surveys, so
that the ministry of our church remains relevant
to the changing needs of our community.
Establish and maintain a 10-year vision & plan.
Discern future worship experiences.*

After serving as the interims, Bruce and Kathy Beardsley were welcomed back with open arms as the permanent Ministers of Music, the position they had held before their leave. Around the same time Sarah Culp's returned to her position on a part time basis.

In May IUCC hosted a musical entitled "Mama's Mansion," put on by the Women of the Well with music provided by members of the Irondequoit United Church of Christ under the direction of Kathy Beardsley. This was a musical parable with stories of women from scripture and tradition. Then what a wonderful idea it was in June of 2002 to present the Reunion Choir, in which everyone who had participated at any time in the music program was invited to sing together.

IUCC continued its journey into the 21st century by addressing church areas in need of attention.  Issues they addressed included the need for a new sound system for the sanctuary, balcony and corridors; and looking for a new full-time layperson to coordinate groups and activities.

One important group issue came about as a result of Colleen Curry's departure and Sarah Culp's half-time status. The Church and Ministry Committee and the Board of Trustees had been in consultation with the Vision Team and Pastor Dale to identify staffing needs as the church prepared to move into a new era of ministry and faith. The proposal was for a full-time pastor, a one-third-time associate pastor responsible for pastoral care, and a full-time, non-ordained person responsible for the coordination, development and promotion of small-group activities.

In an effort to move ahead with the identified areas, the Memorial Committee agreed to fund a new sound system for the sanctuary.  The Capital Funds Campaign underwrote the repair and replacement of the steps and columns at the church's front entry.  In addition, IUCC became one of six churches that had applied for a grant from the Lilly foundation to learn how a church can organize into small groups, as a congregation that is "willing to try new things."

In July IUCC was selected as one of forty pilot congregations throughout the United States for a twenty-four-month process geared toward helping thoughtful Christians discern their unique giftedness and to understand that giftedness in the larger context of faithful discipleship. This was a way to come closer to finding God's work for each person in this world without necessarily feeling like one has to become a "church worker" in order to be faithful or faith-filled.

The traditional Chicken Barbecue continued to be a success in October, growing in attendance each year. This event takes the dedication of the leaders who organize the pick-up and purchase of the food and the soliciting of volunteers to cook, serve and present the food to the customers who come to enjoy the meal.

In November the church welcomed Howard Friend, a renowned author and respected theologian. Dr. Friend's 1998 book, *Recovering the Sacred Center*, is one of the leading literary works devoted to helping individuals and congregations live more God-centered, purposeful lives. The weekend commenced with a Friday evening event entitled "Journey to the Sacred Center," followed by a Saturday retreat at the Webster United Church of Christ and ending in

Sunday morning worship at IUCC. The event was free to all who wished to attend.

By December of 2002 the search was on for a Director of Small Groups.  The full-time, salaried position required someone with the ability to promote and communicate a small-group emphasis throughout the faith community.

Just as important was the ongoing project to create a Vision Statement.

The church involvements of the past, along with the new areas of involvement called for some changes and IUCC made the determination to support but not be a sponsor for the local Habitat for Humanity project.

On February 20, 2003 the announcement was made that the Director of Small Communities had been selected and would be greeted at a reception on Sunday Feb. 23. Jenna Barnardi was introduced, to the congregation and spent the next few months getting to know the church family and the role she would play.

***

The church began 2003 going forward with all the changes presented during the previous year as well as participation in our traditional yearly projects.

The children put on a skit entitled "*Umbrella Man*". There was the appeal to support the Sunset House 5K Run and Fitness Walk in May, the review of proposals for the replacement of columns and steps, the September retreat, this year to be held at Hamlin Beach Park, and the Strawberry Festival and Chicken Barbecue.

A summer music camp was held with the theme "100% Change of Rain."

In June a special handbell performance was given for the community at large. Not to be overlooked was the youth group 30-Hour Famine that had become a yearly event.  By September work began on the church columns and steps to bring them back to their original beauty.

## Rochester Area Interfaith Hospitality Network (RAIHN)

One addition to church outreach was the signing of the Covenant for Hosting the Rochester Area Interfaith Hospitality Network (RAIHN). The mission of RAIHN is to provide temporary accommodations, food and compassionate friendship to families in the Rochester area who have lost their homes. RAIHN is a network of host and support organizations (interdenominational faith communities), which are led by a Rochester-based non-profit corporation and board of directors. The Interfaith Hospitality Network benefits guests in the program as well as the faith-community congregations and volunteers who help.

To the guests in the program, a day in the life of RAIHN provides shelter from the storm. To the organizations and their volunteers, a day in the life of RAIHN is an uplifting and worthwhile experience. A total of thirteen host faith communities was needed to set the program in motion, and by December 2003 the count was at eleven.

On October 19, 2003, Jim Hinman, IUCC Moderator, Jeannie Gloss, Acting Coordinator for RAIHN, and the Rev. Dale Davis made IUCC's involvement official, and in April 2004 IUCC opened its doors to the first RAIHN guests.

Jim Hinman, Jeanne Gloss & Rev Davis sign the RAIHN papers

A maximum of fourteen people or up to five families can be hosted at once. Because of the size of IUCC's facilities, each family was able to be housed in separate Sunday school rooms.  Since beds are part of the system supplies that follow the families from church to church, accommodations were available to temporarily furnish each room.

## Irondequoit Community Cupboard

The Board of Outreach voted to support the Irondequoit Community Cupboard, which was a rechanneling of support that had been sent to the Community Food Cupboard of Rochester on Clinton Avenue.  The Irondequoit Community Cupboard, Inc. is a not-for-profit organization designed to meet a variety of needs for families and individuals in the Town of Irondequoit.

The "concept" of Irondequoit Community Cupboard, Inc. began in 1995. Debbie Evans, an Irondequoit resident, was an active volunteer in the East Irondequoit school district and noticed several children who didn't have winter clothes to wear. She found that there were many families living right in her own community who were living without basic necessities; food, clothes, hygiene items, etc.

What started out as helping a few families in 1995 with a PTA sponsored "Hat, Coat and Boot Exchange" in 1996 has grown into a New York State not-for-profit organization.

When the Board learned that over forty per cent of the children in the East Irondequoit School District qualified for the food programs, IUCC determined support in the community was necessary.

The Irondequoit United Church of Christ began to send volunteers to help at the cupboard as well as be a collection place for food donations to be taken to the cupboard.

## The Ibrahim Family

Keeping with the past efforts to help those less fortunate than ourselves continued.

Excitement was high for the arrival of a Somali Bantu refugee family that a committee of eight IUCC members, chaired by Jeannie and David Gloss, was sponsoring through the Catholic Family Center.

The Ibrahim family, devout Muslims, arrived on April 1, 2004. In preparation for their arrival, donations of clothing and furniture were made, and a team of twenty tutors was trained to teach the family English and American culture. Because they had had no schooling in Africa, they were illiterate even in their own language. The children were immediately registered in public school, and the adults were sent to the Family Learning Center. After a few months, the father, Siraji, began working as a groundskeeper at Holy Sepulchre Cemetery. The church continued to offer any and all assistance necessary to make the family comfortable.

***

The church was moving in the right direction, reflecting feelings expressed in an article from a 1898 issue of "The Aggressive Christian" that contained a story relating to the history of the Irondequoit Union Sunday school:

Irondequoit people are industrious, prosperous and markedly religious. No more delightful community can be found. Its religious organizations are unique. It stands alone as the model for union and cooperation of a denomination in worship and work. All the years these denominations have dwelt together as brethren in perfect fellowship and harmony.

Fully as important to the life and growth of the Sunday school has been the remarkable devotion to its work given by many individuals and by many families over long periods of time. The long terms of service of officers and teachers, the many extraordinary attendance records and most of all the persistence throughout the ten decades of the same familiar names all attest the deep abiding faith which inspired those who laid the foundations, which encouraged those who built so well and the heritage of which should guide United Congregational Sunday School through another hundred years of purposeful service in Irondequoit.

In May 2004 the Rev. and Mrs. Robert Bermudes returned to Rochester for a visit. He served as guest speaker for the Mother's Day Sunday service that year and received a standing ovation

Before the end of May, a newspaper headline read, "They'll be racing around Irondequoit Saturday" as IUCC and the Town of Irondequoit played host to the third running of the Sunset House 5K road race.

Summer would not be summer without the annual Strawberry Festival, that had proven to be a success each year since its inception. With the culmination hard work and dedication, the volunteers and organizers worked hard toward making each year's festival better than the one before. This would be IUCC's twenty-fourth Strawberry Festival.

It was a time of remembrance as the year unfolded and one remembrance that took place for the first time was the opportunity to recognize and congratulate those people of IUCC who had been members for fifty years or more. It is surprising just how many members by the year 2004 had been members of the church for 50 plus years. It was indeed an acknowledge worth celebrating.

| The 2004 Fifty Plus Members | | |
|---|---|---|
| **First/Maiden & Last Name** | | **Start Date** |
| Patricia | Adams | 12/5/54 |
| Robert | Allen | 6/4/48 |
| Eleanor Brown | Bell | 4/14/35 |
| Mahlon | Blake | 6/7/53 |
| Barbara | Bullock | 10/3/54 |
| Jerrod\ | Bullock | 10/3/54 |
| Helen | Crayton | 4/2/44 |
| Wilford | Crayton | 4/2/44 |

| The 2004 Fifty Plus Members | | |
|---|---|---|
| **First/Maiden & Last Name** | | **Start Date** |
| Caroline Rudman | Crumrine | 3/29/42 |
| Frances | Edwards | 10/5/52 |
| Thomas | Edwards | 10/5/52 |
| John | Fulton | 2/4/52 |
| Everett | Gardner | 3/30/47 |
| Maurice T. | Gerks | 4/2/44 |
| Pearl | Hess | 2/6/49 |
| Helen Stubbs | Hulse | 4/1/38 |
| Blanche | Johnson | 2/3/47 |
| Diana | Kubick | 2/1/53 |
| Harry | Kubick | 2/1/53 |
| Neil | Lawrence | 3/29/42 |
| Ruth Holley | Leusch | 6/1/52 |
| Carol | Loveland | 6/6/54` |
| James | Loveland | 6/6/54 |
| Ruth Newman | MacGregor | 4/2/22 |
| Geraldine | Neff | 10/3/54 |
| Warren | Neff | 10/3/54 |
| Effie | Partridge | 6/4/50 |
| Sylvester | Partridge | 6/4/50 |
| Samuel | Pell | 3/18/51 |
| Lorene | Phillips | 3/31/46 |
| David | Richey | 6/3/51 |
| Ruth | Scudder | 4/2/44 |
| Dorothy | Smallridge | `6/3/45 |
| Ann Vaisey | Smith | 3/31/46 |
| Bernice | Stanton | 1/6/46 |
| Evelyn | Stateler | 4/2/50 |
| Jack | Stateler | 4/2/50 |
| Howard | Trimby | 3/18/51 |
| Charles | Turner, Jr. | 6/4/44 |
| Mark | VanDussen | 12/14/49 |
| Kay | VanDussen | 12/14/49 |
| Nilva Coutts | Viken | 4/2/39 |

What better way to end the year than being entertained by the children who, at the 2004 Christmas service, presented the play, "*The 12 Days Of Christmas*."

*****

In 2005 RAIHN had proven to be a successful venture with leaders such as Jeannie and David Gloss, Nancy and Al Smith, Joni

Hinman, Elaine Hiscock, Mary Kay Bradley, Cathy Kwit, Andy Ludwig (St. John's) and Peg David (Seneca Methodist Church). Their call for blankets, mattresses and food were fulfilled, making the families comfortable during their stay. When RAIHN started, thirteen churches were in the circuit, but by 2005 the number was fifteen, which eased the schedule and having five support congregations helping out helped improve service to the families.

## The Guidance Document

Changes that had been under discussion for the church family were summarized in the Guidance Document, which was presented to the congregation for discussion. The Guidance Document replaced the Constitution and By-laws of the Irondequoit United Church of Christ, which was adopted on May 19, 1996.

A thank you was extended to Nita Tischendorf for her promptness and efficiency in producing the finalized document for distribution.  This would then be the way that the IUCC would move forward in the present.


Each year new causes that needed IUCC's help were explored. In 2005 the Peacemaking Focus Group offered aid to victims in Nicaragua after Hurricane Katrina, in what was the costliest hurricane and one of the five deadliest in the history of the United States.

In an effort to keep current on the group participation in IUCC, an Activities Book was created. On a yearly basis, the book reports what each group has accomplished during the year.

The dedication of IUCC members is tireless and courageous, and no better example can be found than our own Helen Rice,  Helen has no bounds as she provides help where ever needed as this Senior Spotlight article attest.

## Senior Spotlight

# Recipe for a Servant-Leader

**By Reverend Dale Davis**
*Pastor of Irondequoit United Church of Christ*

On Sunday, November 21st, over three hundred Irondequoiters gathered in prayer and to share a Thanksgiving feast. Every year, one Irondequoit faith community takes the role of coordinating the community Thanksgiving Worship and Dinner. This year, the honor was given to my congregation, the Irondequoit United Church of Christ (IUCC).

The thought of coordinating Thanksgiving dinner for over three hundred people may seem daunting, but IUCC had one important asset — Helen Rice. Helen Rice is no ordinary person. At age 93, she has the energy of a twenty-something and commands the respect of her congregation without equal.

Helen is the first person to tell you it was a crew of seventy IUCC members who deserve the credit. They did it all— purchased the food, cooked and baked, served and cleaned-up. Not surprisingly, the crew under Helen's direction served 345 people in about twenty minutes!!!!

Who is this 93 year old dynamo? She is retired from Irondequoit High School where she worked for 39 years as librarian. She is an avid bird watcher, peace activist and world traveler. She is very conscious of the less fortunate and with IUCC's Women's Fellowship, Helen makes school bags and quilts for third world countries and the poor in the US.

When asked why she does so much, Helen replies "It's my faith which tells me to show God's love. And, God's love tells me I should be concerned for the peace, welfare and wellbeing of others." Irondequoit and the world are blessed because of Helen Rice.

In 2005, keeping with her hopes to initiate a trend to reach out in nontraditional ways, Jenna Rickey Bernardi, the Director of Small Communities, presented a music jam session during her second year at IUCC. It was an interesting way to draw the community into IUCC.

Two Thousand and Five was a year when the Endowment Fund and the General Funds of the church were enriched by several donations that included $16,000 from the estate of Leslie L. Clarke, $141,146.75 from the estate of Grace Hickson, and $20,176.14 from the estate of John Mackey.

Last sponsored in 1999, IUCC again invited the African Children's Choir to present their unique message in song again in 2005.

Church members provided housing and meals for the children, who performed songs accompanied by drums and ethnic instruments.

One cannot ignore the birthdays of long-time members. Syl Partridge's reaching the one hundred mark in 2005 was a time to celebrate. Syl and his wife, Effie (age ninety-nine) called Irondequoit home for seventy-one years of their marriage.

Syl and Effie have been active members of IUCC as far back as anyone can recall. It was no surprise to anyone that the celebration continued for days, including a special performance by Robert Dalton who played the bagpipes in front of their home. The Partridges shared their live with four daughters: Betty Jane, Barbara Joan, Judy and Patricia.

In 2005 Women's Fellowship hosted a four-part series to raise people's consciousness of the AIDS pandemic in sub-Saharan Africa, which is swallowing families, communities and hopes. So far 17 million have died, and least 25 million may follow.  The IUCC program provided an intimate look at this modern curse. To bring the issue home, the following commentary was designed.

> *You get up in the morning and breakfast*
> *with your three kids. One is already doomed*
> *to die in infancy. Your husband works 200*
> *miles away, comes home twice a year and*
> *sleeps around in between. You risk your life*
> *in every act of sexual intercourse. You go to*
> *work past a house where a teenager lives*
> *alone tending young siblings without any*
> *source of income. At another house, the*
> *wife was branded a whore when she asked*
> *her husband to use a condom, beaten silly*
> *and thrown into the streets. Over there lies*
> *a man desperately sick without access to a*
> *doctor or clinic or medicine or food or*
> *blankets or even a kind word. At work you*
> *eat with colleagues, and every third one is*
> *already fatally ill. You whisper about a*
> *friend who admitted she had the plague and*
> *whose neighbors stoned her to death. Your*
> *leisure is occupied by the funerals you*
> *attend every Saturday. You go to bed*
> *fearing adults your age will not live into*
> *their 40s. You and your*
> *neighbors and your political and popular*
> *leaders act as if nothing is happening.*

It was putting the need in perspective that helped raise funds to do our part in trying to find a cure for this disease.

This year marked the need for an updated church directory and hopes that the full church body would have their pictures taken individually and as a group so that all appeared in the directory. The day for the group picture was bright and sunny, making for an excellent shot done on the front steps of the church.

On October 7,
2005, Raymond Jacobson
passed, leaving his wife
Evie, who honored him by
presenting the church with
a picture that hangs in the
church foyer. Ray and
Evie were long-standing
and involved members of
the church.  Evie, an artist,
drew the picture, making it
a very special memorial.

Continuing to bring IUCC into the future, in November of 2005
the Guidance Document was presented to the congregation and
adopted.

***

A church the size of the IUCC was always in need of special
attention in one area or another.  One of the major issues presented to
the Church Council in 2006 was the need for organ repairs, and funds
were earmarked for this expensive and necessary project.  It was
around this time that discussions on changes in the sanctuary were also
under consideration.  What stopped any action was the need for funds
to meet the expenses that would be incurred.

## Tidbits Of The Year 2006

The Bantu Family delivered a healthy baby girl in February.
This was also the year that IUCC's Small Groups Community leader,
Jenna Bernardi, announced she would be leaving. Her efforts had gone
far in establishing small communities that were beneficial to the church
and to the community.

The leadership council awaited bids for the master plan
development identified by the committee to redesign and repair the
church building. The two architects, Sean Moran and John Bero, had
been approached with the plan. The job that Sean Moran would begin

to undertake at this stage was engaging ministry groups that use or could use the sanctuary to solicit more input on how the current space met or was unable to meeting their worship and ministry needs.

Around the same time, Pastor Dale announced he would be taking a sabbatical from April through June. During this period he would research the means by which traditional, mainline Protestant congregations in the Northeast have grown through cultural changes that have left most churches like ours in a declining state of membership and resources for ministry. The church was looking at creating memorable services and studying other issues—the reason for the new Ministry Plan Implementation and the updates made in 2006. During his sabbatical, the worship services were planned and conducted by lay leadership.

In March of 2006 funds for the sanctuary upgrade were secured, but the Leadership Council voted to begin with the overall property instead of the sanctuary-upgrade plan. As a startup, the choir stalls and the pulpit were removed from the chancel. Randy MacDonald was hired to do the removal and place these items in storage. Meetings with the congregation were held to determine their feelings for the physical changes that were being suggested for the sanctuary. At the meetings it was explained that the architect fee would not exceed $15,000 and that the reason for the changes were for the approaching one hundredth anniversary of the sanctuary building, which was showing its age. The church budget included $85,000 per year just to keep the building open. The building infrastructure was in need of an overall upgrade—electrical, plumbing and heating—and repairs were needed to the parking lot and roof. Because there was more recognized areas for attention and not enough funds to go around, everything was put on hold.

Quilts made by the Material Aides Group were sent to Church World Services (CWS).  Before the quilts were to ship out, the Material Aides Group displayed them at the windows of the sanctuary.

CWS is people reaching out to neighbors in need near and far. They work with partners in the U.S. and around the world to build interfaith and intercultural coalitions to eradicate hunger and poverty and promote peace and justice.

Pat Partridge initiated and successfully concluded a "20-to-40 age group" dinner, representing another of IUCC's congregational outreaches that met with positive results.

The success of a joint venture of IUCC and the Islamic Center of Rochester's program of Islam 101 was another innovative and successful event.

***

Sean Moran, architect with Dewolff Partnership Architects, was unanimously selected by the Physical Resource Team for his visionary planning for the church updates. At this point, the interest was in going forward with the plans.  Dewolff Partnership Architects would guide the church through the process of evaluating sanctuary use and recommend enhancements to make it work better for everyone.

In June of 2006 Herbert Partridge (Syl) passed away at age one hundred. Married for seventy-two years to his wife Effie, they had been involved members of the Irondequoit United Church of Christ for many years.

Around this time the church engaged Laura Hood as the Consultant for Christian Education and Youth Programs.  The Sunday school hours were among the changes she was considering. In an effort to shorten the time commitment that families previously had on Sunday mornings, the young children would attend Sunday school at the same time the older youth and adults were in morning worship.

The year of 2006 saw Kathy and Bruce Beardsley taking an eight-week hiatus. During that period they planned to visit other churches that held alternative and traditional worship services and see how we could best incorporate this seemingly new trend. We live in an era when people seek options, and it is important to respond with worship opportunities providing a choice of style, hour and location.

Worship is the primary purpose of any Christian Church and forms the core of our congregation's life together. It motivates us to accomplish God's purposes and to minister to His people. It forms the opportunity we have to respond to the marvelous grace God has given us in Jesus Christ. Worship services with a vital music ministry adds energy and meaning to the service and worship in two styles were becoming quite common.  Each style was Christ-centered, and biblically-based.

Kept in mind was that worship styles can affect everything from the music choices and selections, as well as how and with what instruments they are played. Worship Styles are also affected by how the pastor presents God's Word or the message. In the "world of worship" services, there are basically two types of worship styles. "Traditional" and "Contemporary"

# Contemporary Worship Service

This means that there is most likely no choir involved. Instead you'll have a "praise & worship team". This team will usually consist of a singer or two, a guitar or keyboard, a set of drums, and in larger churches all of the above. The music will usually consist of newer styles written by newer artists. On occasions "oldies" are included. In larger churches overhead screens will display the lyrics to assist the congregation in singing. The pastor will speak afterwards, and the terms preacher, pastor, and minister are interchangeable. This is also true with Traditional styles.

# Traditional Worship Service

In a Traditional Worship service you will typically have a choir and a choir leader or director. The choir will typically sing in unison with the congregation using hymnals. The hymnal, by the way, is that book which is usually sitting right next to you or directly in front of you during the service. The song selection can vary, but will usually consist of more traditional hymns. Some that come to mind are "I'll Fly Away", "Amazing Grace", or "Just As I Am". A piano, organ, or keyboard will assist as an accompaniment. Again as stated before, the preacher will present God's Message afterwards.

There was much discussion along the vein that to separate the congregation would put a rift in the church itself. As time passed the congregation began to see this as a way to offer to each member, the type of service they wished to attend. In this way it kept the church family together.

In the end the names for the styles would change.

# Web Ministry

Web ministry is any and every way that your church can or could reach out to members, visitors, seekers and leaders through a variety of Web and Internet technology tools. Most people think of Web ministry as having a website, but there is so much more to developing and maintaining a dynamic Web ministry for your local church, district or conference organization. In fact, Web ministry should be just as prominent and integrated into your congregation or organization's total ministry plan as any other aspect.

Web ministry adapts the tools of the Internet and resources of the world-wide Web to fulfill the church's mission of making disciples of Jesus Christ for the transformation of the world. It makes use of the vast communication and information cyber-highway to connect with billions of people.

The first meeting to begin implementation of the IUCC Web Ministry took place on August 13. Led by Kevin Branch, the design, content and timeline were addressed.

The VISION of the Irondequoit United Church of Christ (IUCC) is to know and love God personally, through relationships, the use of our gifts, and reaching out to others.

To achieve our Vision, we commit ourselves to creating an environment of dedication to God through worship, prayer, fellowship, learning, and following the living Christ. This is the PURPOSE of IUCC.

Our CURRENT STRENGTHS and CORE VALUES are:

**We deeply value our relationships with each other and God.** It is at the center of who we are.

**We care for children and youth.** We are invested in sharing the experience of Christ and his teachings.

**We celebrate individual and group vocation.** Each of us offers special and unique gifts.

**We reach out to the community and world.** It is an important part of our mission of being outwardly focused.

**We are an intellectual seeking church.** We understand that reformation and change helps make our faith relevant, exciting, and personal.

**We share the love of music and the arts.** Its various styles and forms strengthen our faith.

**We live as a focused and forward thinking congregation.** We organize and structure ourselves around our vision, and empower individuals and groups in all their callings.

Our connection to the **HISTORY** of the Christian Church recognizes God the creator, Jesus Christ as Savior, and looks to the guidance of the Holy Spirit and the Bible in order to live more fully as members of Christ's body on earth. We claim as our inheritance the Church of Jesus Christ since its creation. We acknowledge the legacy and guidance of the Church as it moved through reformation and change. We affirm our responsibility to make the Church of Jesus Christ relevant to our day and age while preserving the core understandings of the Christian faith. We recognize two sacraments: Baptism and the Lord's Supper. We encourage each member to interpret the scripture under the guidance of the Holy Spirit. We have a covenantal relationship with the United Church of Christ.

Uniting ourselves in Christian fellowship, we COVENANT with one another to:

Worship God in everything we do every day of our lives.

Share our spiritual gifts with each other and with the community.

Help each other discover and grow our callings in Christ.

Live the gospel of Jesus Christ in the community and the world.

Our POLITY is to follow the rich history of the United Church of Christ, in which IUCC is governed by the members of the congregation while observing the faith and order of the United Church of Christ and the religious incorporation laws of the State of New York.

The Irondequoit United Church of Christ welcomes all people who want to participate in its community no matter where they are in their faith journey. The church is governed by MEMBERS who have pledged themselves to the life and body of IUCC.

**Members** and other **participants** are encouraged to actively engage in any aspect of the IUCC's worship, education, fellowship, small communities, music, outreach, stewardship, and other spiritual and personal growth opportunities.

Each year, IUCC will ask participants and members to recommit themselves to the journey of the church. This enables each one to know the church community better, and help achieve its vision.

All members of IUCC are also members of the United Church of Christ.

Because we deeply value our relationships with each other and God, we reaffirm and strengthen them through WORSHIP.

Services of worship shall be celebrated regularly on Sundays. Other services of worship will take place based upon tradition (Christmas Eve, Maundy Thursday) and the needs of the congregation (alternative worship services, healing services).

The Sacrament of the Lord's Supper, or Holy Communion, shall be celebrated based upon tradition and the needs of the congregation. The Sacrament of Baptism, either of children or adults, may be observed upon request and in consultation with the pastor.

Every group in the church, with the exception of the Leadership Council, is considered a **SMALL COMMUNITY** (a.k.a. "small group"). Small communities provide the primary means for experiencing authentic Christian community by providing opportunities that include learning, caring, serving and prayer.

Some groups will focus primarily on learning, in order to help people grow in their faith and apply the gospel to daily living (e.g. bible study, book discussions, video series, speakers).

Some groups will focus primarily on caring, in order to provide mutual care and support to group members who share a common need or concern (e.g. support groups, prayer groups, visitation groups).

Some groups will focus primarily on serving, in order to provide opportunities for people with similar interests to work together in service to others (e.g. outreach ministries, worship teams, service projects).

Small Communities:

Meet together on a regular basis.

Allow anyone to Participate (church member or not) at any time.

Have no nominations or elections. People choose to participate in small communities that relate to their particular needs and interests.

Determine how long, how frequently, and where, they will meet. Some groups will decide to be ongoing, some will decide to meet for a specific number of weeks, and some will decide to meet until a particular project or process is completed.

Have a responsibility to appropriately communicate the times, dates, and purpose of their meetings to the congregation.

Have a purpose consistent with the vision and values of the Irondequoit United Church of Christ.

The LEADERSHIP COUNCIL works together to support pursuing our Vision & Purpose through success of Worship and Small Communities. It is composed of:

Church President

Vision Team

Physical Resource Team

People Resource Team

The Leadership Council shall meet together no less than quarterly to:

Develop a ministry plan for the coming year to present to the congregation at the November Congregational meeting. The ministry plan shall reflect the vision, core values, and mission priorities of IUCC and identify the opportunities and challenges important to address in the coming year.

Review progress and address challenges in implementing the congregation's ministry plan.

Plan Congregational Meetings.

Transact business and set policy referred by any of the three teams.

Review and/or approve plans from small communities, officers, or other individuals that the Leadership Council or Church President has requested.

Leadership Council shall keep a record of its proceedings on file in the church office.

Except where restricted by the Guidance Document, the Leadership Council shall determine the Standard tenure of officers and any attendance requirements for members of the Leadership Council.

The CHURCH PRESIDENT is the chief operating officer of the Church, presides over the Leadership Council and Steering Team, and with agenda, moves the church process forward. The president, who must be a member of IUCC, is authorized to sign legal documents on behalf of the Church.

The STEERING TEAM ensures continuity of the Ministry Plan. It is composed of five (5) members: Church President (chairperson), Senior Pastor, Vision Team Leader, Physical Resources Team Leader, and the People Resource Team Leader. The members of the Vision, Physical Resources, and People Resource Teams select one of their own as Team Leader and representative to the Steering Team. The primary responsibility of this group is to act as liaison and coordinator between the three Leadership Council teams, the Congregation, and the Professional Staff.

The VISION TEAM ensures the success of Worship and Small Communities by building consensus with the congregation for our Vision, Core values, Mission Priorities, and Long Range Goals. The team works with, and is supported by the professional staff as necessary. It aims to have five (5) elected members with overlapping two-year terms.

The Primary Responsibilities of the team are to:

Continuously review, articulate, and facilitate the process for updating the vision, core values, mission priorities, and long-range goals of our congregation.

Identify the needs of our community through efforts such as public benchmarks and surveys, so that the ministry of our church remains relevant to the changing needs of our community.

Establish and maintain a 10-year vision & plan.

The Physical Resource Team ensures the success of Worship and Small Communities by providing access to needed financial and material resources.   The team works with, and is supported by the professional staff as necessary.  It aims to have seven (7) elected members with overlapping two-year terms.

The Primary Responsibilities of the team are to:

Develop an annual budget that aligns financial resources with the annual ministry plan developed by the Leadership Council and adopted by the congregation.

Allocate financial resources in accordance with the Annual Ministry Plan. (How can we help you?)

Promote Stewardship and oversee an annual campaign.

Discern future worship experiences

Oversee Investments and proceeds of endowment in accordance with the annual ministry plan.

Oversee the care and upkeep of the church facility.

The People Resource Team ensures the success of Worship and Small Communities by equipping leaders and expanding opportunities for people to discern their Gifts and Callings and participate in small communities.  The team works with, and is supported by the professional staff as necessary.  It aims to have seven (7) elected members with overlapping two-year terms.

The Primary Responsibilities of the team are to:

Oversee selection of nominees for president and the three Leadership teams.

Provide leaders for the major ministry plan of the church.

Identify, train, equip, and support leaders of small communities.

Design a process that empowers people to discern and initiate ministries

Ensure training and support for those in ministry.

Develop Magnet Events that attract people with shared interests and needs.

Support active participation of church members

Design a process for those in small communities to:

Schedule activities and facilities

Publicize programs and activities

Additional Responsibilities of the People Resource Team include:

Hiring and termination of employees.

Preparation of contracts for employees.

Overseeing performance Review process

Developing and updating personnel policies and procedures.

Providing confidential and appropriate venue for resolving personnel conflicts and congregational concerns.

Officers Of The Church:

(A description of duties of each officer shall be on file in the church office):

Church President: See above.

Leadership Council Vice-President: The Leadership Council Vice-President is elected from the membership of the Leadership Council and shall preside over the Leadership Council in the absence of the president.

Clerk*:* The Church Clerk shall record the proceedings of all church body and Leadership Council meetings, and conduct all correspondence not otherwise provided for.

Treasurer*:* The Treasurer shall receive direction from the Physical Resource Team.  The Treasurer is responsible for all financial transactions of the church and also oversees the financial secretary, endowment fund treasurer, and memorial treasurer.

Financial Secretary*:* The Secretary shall receive direction from the Treasurer.

Endowment Fund Treasurer: The Treasurer shall receive direction from the Treasurer.

***Memorial Treasurer:*** The Treasurer shall receive direction from the Treasurer.

***Auditor or Audit Team:*** The Auditor or Audit Team shall conduct an annual examination of the financial books and records of the church. The Auditor or Audit Team shall provide a report of finances and a report of internal controls and procedures to the Physical Resource Team.

Elections:

Election of Leadership Council*:*

The Leadership Council (Including the Church President and members of each of Vision, Physical Resource and People Resource Teams) shall be elected by a majority vote at the Annual Meeting of the Congregation on or about the third Sunday in May. It is the right of any voting member of the Congregation to nominate any church member as a candidate. Nomination will take the form of a paragraph stating why the nominee is appropriate for the office.

Members of the Council serve two-year terms that commence upon election.

The number of terms an individual may serve is determined by two factors:

The desirability of turnover for fresh ideas, insights, and opportunity.

"Calling" of an individual into a particular vocation or service.

If a member serves more than 2 years, he/she must be re-elected to do so.

If vacancies occur among the officers of the Leadership Teams, the Leadership Council shall fill them for the unexpired term.

Election of Officers*:*

The Church Clerk and Treasurer shall be church members elected to office by a majority vote at the Annual Meeting as noted above.  They shall serve two-year terms of office.

The following officers shall be church members elected to office by the Leadership Council: Vice-President (from existing membership of Leadership Council), Financial Secretary, Treasurer, Auditor or Audit Team, Endowment Fund Treasurer, and Memorial Treasurer.

Election of Pastor and other Professional Staff:

The president in consultation with the leadership Council shall appoint a Search Committee to seek a candidate for Pastor.

The Search Committee shall follow the guidelines published by the United Church of Christ to organize and conduct the search process.

The Search Committee shall present to the Congregation the name of the candidate it recommends to fill the vacancy. A vote of two-thirds majority of the Governing Body shall be required.

A contract for professional staff shall be approved by the Leadership Council, and signed by the president and professional hire.

The pastor, People Resource Team, and Area Conference Minister shall receive copies of the contract.

A process for termination shall be included in the contract. In the event of a termination, the Chairperson of the Leadership Council shall send notice to the Area Conference Minister for appropriate action.

Discipline of the Pastor(s) shall be in conformity with Association Guidelines.

Other Procedures:

Church Body Meetings:

The governing body of the church shall be the membership assembled in a meeting of the church body.  Meetings shall be open to all members of the church.

A meeting shall be held in October to receive the ministry plan from the Leadership Council.

A meeting shall be held before the end of February to receive financial reports and to adopt a budget.

A meeting shall be held in May to receive annual reports and to conduct elections for the Leadership Council and other officers as necessary.

A special meeting may be called for other church business as needed. The Physical Resource Team shall call a meeting at the request of the Leadership Council, the Senior Pastor, at least ten members of the church or by its own action.

Notices for all corporate meetings shall be given in accordance with the requirements of NYS law.

The presence of at least fifty (50) members of the church shall constitute a quorum for the conduct of business.

Property:

The Church may, in its corporate name, sue or be sued; acquire by purchase, gift, device, bequest or otherwise, and own, hold, invest, reinvest, or dispose of property, both real and personal, for such work as the church may undertake; and may purchase, own, receive, hold, manage, care for and transfer, rent, lease, mortgage, or otherwise encumber, sell, assign transfer, or convey such property for the general purposes of the Church. It may receive and hold in trust both real and personal property, and invest and reinvest the same, and make any contracts for promoting the objects and purposes of the Church.

Upon dissolution of the Church, its assets and all property and interests of which it shall then be possessed, including any devise, bequest, gift, or grant contained in any will or other instrument, in trust of otherwise, made before or after such dissolution, shall be transferred to the New York State Conference of the United Church of Christ, or such other entity or religious corporation as the members of the church may determine at a duly called congregational meeting).

Rules Of Order:

Roberts Rules of Order shall be the Parliamentary authority for all matters of procedure not specifically covered in this Guidance Document.

Amendments:

Amendments to this Guidance Document may be made at any duly called meeting of the members of the church by a vote of two-thirds majority of those present. Public announcement of the proposal to amend this Document shall be made at least thirty days prior to the vote and the text of the amendment(s) shall be published, posted, and available for study.

Small groups continued to be a source of outreach to the church and the community at large with new groups forming regularly and old groups being revisited.

In September 2006, the Women's Breakfast small community was established. The group scheduled to meet the second Saturday of each month at 9:00 a.m. at the East Ridge Family Restaurant in Irondequoit.

The Strawberry Festival and the Larry Clarke Chicken Barbecue—named in honor of an active, long-standing member who had recently passed away—continued to attract record numbers, requiring more volunteers and more time to arrange each year's event. These two events became a time to enjoy music, reconnect with old friends, meet new members and greet church neighbors and community guests, all while adding revenue for IUCC budget needs.

## The Adoption of the Ministry Plan

*The way to achieve success is first to have a definite clear practical -- a goal, an objective.  Second have the necessary* *means to achieve your ends-- wisdom, money, materials and methods. Third adjust your means to that end.  **Aristotle***

In keeping with the format, the team worked on the layout of the ministry plan and the proposed IUCC 2007 Ministry Plan was passed at a Congregational Meeting. This proposed ministry plan was submitted to the congregation on December 10, 1006. The format of the proposed Ministry plan was outlined as follows:

---

**PROPOSED**
**IUCC 2007 Ministry Plan**

**Develop Spiritual Capacity**
    Practice The Six Marks Of Discipleship
        As A Congregation
        Individually
**Develop Additional Leadership**
    Educational Leadership Course
**Make Our Gatherings Memorable**
    Offer Choice Of Worship Alternatives
        Begin A Second Service
    Enhance Small Groups For All Ages
**Develop A Master Plan For Our Future**
    Total Site Perspective For Mission And Ministry

---

In December, under the Beardsley's' direction, the church put on "The Winter Star," a Christmas mini-musical in which the children represented the first true believers in the star and  the angels.

***

On January 25, 2007 the Irondequoit United Church of Christ hosted a Rochester Philharmonic Orchestra "Around The Town" concert with conductor Eric Townell and violinist Juliana Athayde.

Hundreds of people filled the sanctuary, including the aisles, balcony and lobbies of the church for this free RPO concert.

## Implementing The New Worship Program

In September 2007 IUCC launched an exciting change to worship by offering two distinct services every Sunday. The church added a 9:30 a.m. Celebration Service consisting of contemporary and casual music, drama and visual aids, followed by an 11:00 a.m. Classic Service with more traditional music and delivery. Preschoolers through sixth-graders join the adults for the start of the worship and then were escorted to their classrooms for Sunday school.

On the first Sunday of each month at both services Communion is served.  Trying to foresee problems that might surface, a half-hour fellowship period was instituted between the services for refreshments and fellowship so the unity of the church could prevail.

The IUCC Praise Band had been playing together for almost a year, led by Nathan Padgett, a recent Eastman School of Music graduate and the Music Director. The band had a list of fifty contemporary Christian songs in their repertoire. Each Sunday during the Celebration Service the band played. The congregation was encouraged to do what the spirit and music moves them to do, whether it be sitting and listening or standing, clapping and singing along.

## Taking Part In Change

Small study groups at IUCC reached out to welcome new members. One such group formed was the Way of Forgiveness study group. Companions in Christ: The Way of Forgiveness (Participant's Book), A Small-Group Experience in Spiritual Formation was written by Marjorie J. Thompson. The book states that it takes a lot of willingness and practice to see life from God's perspective. Perhaps nothing goes more against the grain of human nature than the ideas of forgiving those who wound us and accepting forgiveness from others. Using the second release in the Companions in Christ Series, The Way of Forgiveness explores how to deal with these issues to preserve "the beauty of our souls" and to fulfill the teachings of Jesus in the Sermon on the Mount.

# IUCC Spirit Website Is Born

Still moving ahead to identify and meet changing needs and styles of connection, in 2007 the IUCC opened its own website at iuccspirit.com. The website was created to not only have a presence on the internet, but also as a means of getting information to the congregation as well as the community. IUCC's communication avenues had expanded to include—the website (iuccspirit.com), email (iucc@msn.com) and the Lighted Cross.

As it has in the past, the Irondequoit United Church of Christ welcomed children ages three and up to Sunday school throughout the summer. Renamed "Children's Worship Camp," children had fun exploring Bible stories through crafts, songs, games and more while their parents relaxed and recharged at a casual outdoor worship service at 9:30 a.m. (indoors when necessary).

*Irondequoit United Church of Christ*
844 Titus Avenue          Rochester NY 14617

# *The Lighted Cross*

**February 2010**

*Office Hours*
Mon.,Tues.,Thurs.,9 am-4:30 pm
Wednesday, 9 am – Noon
Friday, 8:30 am – 4 pm
Phone: 585-544-3020
Fax:    585-544-3084
E-mail:
office@IUCCspirit.com
Website:
IUCCspirit.com

*Staff:*
Rev. Janice Lee Fitzgerald, Interim Pastor
Robert Bermudes, Pastor Emeritus
Josephine Waser, Office Mgr.
Diana Pratt, Christian

## RECOMMITTING TO THE ONE YOU LOVE

*Renewing Marriage Vows*

Weddings are such an important milestone in one's life. Remember how many details there were to coordinate? Invitations, flowers, party favors, clothes? Those of you who have been married for a while now know that while those things seemed awfully important on your wedding day, it has been the vows that you made that have been of the most lasting importance. Each day of your life, how well you and your spouse have (or have not) been able to live out your promises to each other has been the measure of the strength of your marriage.

Yet, along with the changes, there were some constants such as the sixth annual Sunset House 5K Run and Fitness Walk that was hosted by IUCC in the past and still in the same way. The Director of Sunset House sent a letter to Pastor Dale stating the following:

*"For the past six years, all of you at the Irondequoit United Church of Christ have walked, strolled and run into our hearts here at Sunset House. Each May you have brought together our community to support and celebrate Sunset House and have brought our awareness to so many people the blessings that can come from caring for the dying with understanding, dignity and peace. Each year we are blessed with a tremendously beautiful gift that enables us to continue this care. Thank you and bless you all for our amazing gift of $10,000. You are a very special and loving*

Started in 2006, the second annual combined circle buffet luncheon was held at Murph's. The topic at the luncheon was presented by circle member Jackie Perley, who shared the history of Susan B. Anthony and why without her the women of today would be leading much different lives. Jackie serves as a docent at the Susan B. Anthony house. Members present included Diana Kubick, Effie Partridge, Pat Partridge visible on the left and Nancy Smith, Ann Smith and Laurel Fuller (front to back) on the right.

The Materials Aides Group continued their efforts for Church World Services, providing school bags, baby sets and handmade quilts.

A long-standing group has been the Men's Breakfast group that meets for social get-togethers the second Saturday of the month at the Bayfront restaurant. Pictured here from the left: Bob Allen, Jim Loveland, Jack Stateler, Gerry Leubner, Don Vanselow, Dick Arfman, Jerry Record, David Gloss, Bill Goodman, Harry Kubick and Paul McGurrin.

***

On April 23, 2008, Effie Partridge passed at the age of 101, while visiting her daughter in California. A retired Rochester teacher, she was an avid bridge play and in constant attendance at IUCC.  As an active member of the congregation, she would be very much missed by all.

Just having created and passed the Blueprint for Ministry was reviewed and changed as it attempted to be what the congregation wanted.  A questionnaire was handed out at the Congregational Meeting in May to provide an opportunity for the congregation to review the 2008 Ministry Plan and Blueprint for Ministry's desired outcomes.

This process would equip the congregation with the information needed to ask questions that would help format the finalized version.

## Increased Outreach

For the past several years, the church had been able to increase its Outreach budget. This year was no exception, spreading over $6,000 to help others. IUCC divided the donations as follows:

YMCA, Maplewood Family Branch, to be used in summer youth programs. Foodworx to a ministry for former inmates learning a trade and rejoining the workforce. Salem Nutrition Center to help the poor with bus transportation and food supplies. Community Lutheran Ministry, Inc. for an inner-city children's safe environment and a source of summer camps and religious education. RAIHN for the local Interfaith Hospitality Network, helping IUCC with supplies during the quarterly missions in our church. Alternatives for Battered Women for a group helping women escape harmful relationships. Cameron Community Ministries for an outreach mission in the inner city. Greater Rochester Community of Churches, to bring together all faith communities for ecumenical worship, interfaith dialogue, community ministry, advocacy and service. Project URGE for drawing together people from the faith community with differing backgrounds and a racial diversity to impact existing ministries and agencies with support through volunteering and finances. Eastern Service Workers to an agency helping low-paid urban workers in the inner city. Community Cupboard of Rochester, specializing in helping seniors in the Rochester area. (This is in addition to the food donations placed in the shopping cart by the church office for the Irondequoit Community Food Cupboard.) House of Mercy to a mission on Hudson Avenue for the homeless and hunger.

Global and local outreach by IUCC has included *Water for Sudan,* receiving $300. Water for Sudan, Inc. is a Rochester-based charitable organization operating in Sudan, Africa with a mission to drill fresh-water wells for people in the southern areas of Sudan.

IUCC has also reached out to the *Zululand Hospice,* an outgrowth from a need presented by the Empangeni Rotary Ann's. The Zululand Hospice is committed to serving uMhlathuze Municipality and its environs by providing palliative care for patients with progressive diseases as well as bereavement support for their families.

IUCC also donated to the *India Children's Choir*. These children come from the hills of Manipur in northeast India, along the India-Burma-China border.

Over ninety years ago, the Word of God transformed the Hmar tribe of India from fierce headhunters into Christians.

The India Children's Choir is sponsored by Bibles For The World and is made up of twenty-two children, ages eight to twelve, who are direct descendants of those former headhunters.

The church's long involvement over years of donating to *Church World Service (CWS)* continued through the funding of Material Aids health kit shipping.

*Charles Hall Youth Services* continued to receive donations from IUCC. In 1964, the national United Church of Christ convened a conference of church leaders from reservations in Wisconsin, South Dakota and North Dakota to focus on "What can be done to help broken families and youth in trouble?"

An ongoing donation was sent to *Back Bay Mission*.  Founded in 1922, it is an outreach effort of the First Evangelical Church of Biloxi (later United Church of Christ).

It is a direct result of the UCC churches that Back Bay Mission recovered more quickly than many locally based agencies.

In October of 2008, John Dau visited IUCC.  His message was preceded by some clips from the movie *"God Grew Tired of Us,"* based on his book of the same name. The movie and the book depict the ravages of war in the Sudan that led to the Lost Boys' painful yet faithful journey of more than a decade as refugees, immigrants and now U.S. citizens.

In November IUCC was approached by Edventure; a group sponsored by the No Child Left Behind Act, they provide an after-school program for city youth in the Rochester area. Their mission is to help children reach their potential and realize their dreams through quality education.  They commit to setting new standards in the field of marketing international education. Their vision is to enable and enlighten individuals in the global environment

In 2008 Siraji Abukar Ibrahim, the father in the church's sponsored Bantu family, had surgery for a very aggressive cancer. At his check-up at the end of the year, he learned that the tumor had not metastasized.

While he was in the hospital, his wife, Fatuma, was at the same hospital having a baby. Although the delivery met with complications and the baby was put in an incubator, he is now well. The family is shown in the picture with the new baby, Abukar Abukar (the children take the last name of Abukar even though the parents' last name is Ibrahim).

## Preparing the 2011 Quilt

In 2008, keeping with tradition, Ruth Circle began working the quilt for the church's 100-year celebration. The group has continued to grow and reach out to the community for ways they can serve. One of the mainstays has been the quilt to represent each twenty-five years of the Irondequoit United Church of Christ.

Taking the lead, Lois Metzger began the design for the quilt for the Centennial Year and with the help of members of Ruth Circle, the quilt has become a reality. At the September 15, 2009 meeting, Lois presented the quilt in its final stages of completion. The quilt will have the names of the past ministers embroidered on the base. As has been the tradition, this quilt will represent the body of the church.

Ruth Circle Members Evelyn Stateler & Anne Yeager Put Finishing Touches On The New Quilt.

Ruth Circle Member, Lois Metzger
presents the Centennial Quilt to the members

In an effort to promote the World of Confirmation, Pastor Dale Davis provided the following report on the website.

*Each year young people who are connected to our faith community and who are entering the eighth grade are invited to join a group of their peers for a period of nine months to engage in conversation, learning, serving and reflection. The group meets for two hours each month, and each group member meets with a mentor to talk about matters of faith. This entire process is called confirmation.*

*The word confirmation means "to make firm" or "with firmness." The assumption is that from the time a young person is baptized (usually as an infant) through eighth grade, the faith formation of a young person is formed through family experiences, through teachers and peers in conjunction with the church's children's ministries and through a commitment of a family's participation in the life of a local faith community. Confirmation is merely the work of clarifying and making firm that which has been attended to (or has been in process) for years. The important thing about the confirmation experience is that it represents a beginning—a beginning in terms of how to orient one's life toward God and toward others who also seek to put God at the center of their lives. This year's confirmation experience seeks to equip our young people in these three ways:*

*Help our young people view faith as a journey and not as a possession. Confirmation is not about stuffing information about church into the heads of people with hopes they'll "get it," but is instead equipping each young person to travel with others into the very life of God. It's about formation more than about information.*

*Equip our young people in practicing the habits disciples of Jesus Christ have practiced for centuries and centuries. These habits include learning to pray, making friends with scripture, experiencing the power of small community, discerning how best to serve, readying themselves for worship and celebrating their giftedness.*

*Visit with our young people the 2000-year Tradition of our faith (tradition with a Capital T) and learn about what those who have gone before us have learned about God, Jesus Christ, the power of the Holy Spirit, the church and the world.*

*"That they may all be one' was important to our four original denominations... and is the hallmark of the United Church of Christ today. It reflects our spirit of unity and inclusiveness and points toward future efforts to heal the divisions in the body of Christ."*

***

It was well received when Nathan Padget accepted the position of Director of Music and continue to share his special talents with IUCC and Carol Cowan accepted the position of Organist.

Then, even though it was expected it came as a shock when after nine years of service to IUCC, Pastor Dale Davis announced his departure to become pastor at the Immanuel United Church of Christ in Shillington, Pennsylvania.  Below is a picture of the family (seated from left: Cameron, Helen and Hannah; standing: Pastor Dale).

A farewell luncheon was held on November 9, at which church members shared many fond memories of the previous nine years. The church also presented them with a generous monetary gift from the congregation and a copy of the beautiful Rembrandt painting "The Return of the Prodigal Son," which is one of Pastor Davis' favorites. It was with mixed emotions that members wished them the very best in their new home. We have so much to thank him for during his leadership of IUCC.

His presentation on their website best describes the ministering he offered to IUCC.  Pastor Davis wrote:

*The Church's most central gift is community. We
live in a society where people yearn for deep
community, not just small talk. Yet places where
we can be known for who we really are as well as
have the opportunity to know and celebrate others
is not commonplace. Sometimes you are fortunate
enough to have a workplace or neighborhood or
existing network of friends that gives you a
satisfactory sense of community. Yet even if you do
have such a network you may still find yourself
craving a deeper sense of what it means to be a
human, you may find yourself craving to grow
your spirit, your humanity, your desire to embrace
God. You may even find yourself somewhat alone
while people are all around you.*
*The earliest Christians discovered that despite the
multitude of relationships existing in society, none
could meet their deepest needs quite as well as
fellow believers. They all realized growing closer*

*to God meant growing closer to one another. They
needed a way to do that, however. So they
worshipped together, broke bread in one another's
homes, shared their lives, prayed and celebrated
the abundance of love they'd discovered. They did
it not to form a club of privilege or to simply get
more volunteers to carry out more tasks. Instead,
they realized that if the world was going to
change, it had better start with them. Nothing
fancy, just the desire to seek the Jesus way of
doing things. And the movement caught on.
When I read in the book of Acts about how more
and more people were "saved," I can't help but
think that it means more and more people were
"rescued." Rescued from what? Maybe they were
being rescued from the same kind of stuff we need
to be rescued from: inner loneliness, fear that we
are not putting our best selves to use, boredom,
lack of direction; you name it.
In any case, those early Christians found that
together they could finally embrace that which
had eluded them for so long, a chance to be whole.
The power of a community in Christ is just that,
powerful. I pray that all who have found or will
find the Immanuel United Church of Christ will
find a richness in community like they have never
known before!
Blessings,
Pastor Dale Davis*

## 2009 IUCC Ministry Plan Objectives:

The church welcomed its new Interim Pastor, the Rev. Janice Lee Fitzgerald, on November 10, 2008. She barely had a chance to settle in before she began work on major issues of concern to the church.

At the Annual Financial reports presentation meeting on February 15, 2009, the following Ministry Plan was presented to the full congregation.

1.  **<u>BECOME AN INVITING COMMUNITY</u>**
    ▶ POSSIBILITIES:
        - RADICALLY IMPROVE HOSPITALITY
        - BECOME MORE CHILD FRIENDLY
        - REACH BROADER COMMUNITY
        - CONSIDER CHANGING WORSHIP TIMES
        - BETTER ADVERTISEMENT/PUBLIC RELATIONS
        - IMPROVE APPEARANCE (OUTSIDE AND IN)
        - CONTINUE WITH BLUEPRINT FOR MINISTRY
            - SANCTUARY RENOVATION PLANS
            - BUILDING RENOVATION PLANS

2.  **<u>BEGIN PASTORAL SEARCH PROCESS</u>**
    ▶ A CHURCH WIDE, EVERY MEMBER PROCESS TO ALLOW THE CONGREGATION TO HAVE A VOICE IN THE CHURCH PROFILE
        - CONGREGATIONAL GATHERINGS SCHEDULED
        - CREATE A CHURCH PROFILE FROM GATHERINGS
        - SELECT A SEARCH COMMITTEE
        - MEET WITH DAVE FELTON AND BEGIN THE SEARCH
        - MAY TAKE MORE THAN A YEAR– ON GOD'S TIME

3.  **<u>EXPAND SMALL GROUP PROGRAM</u>**
    ▶ POSSIBILITIES:
        - HIRE A COORDINATOR OR CONSULTANT
        - TRAIN/MENTOR SMALL GROUP LEADERS
        - ENGAGE PEOPLE INSIDE AND OUT OF IUCC
        - DEVELOP MATERIALS
        - ENHANCE VARIETY TO MEET NEEDS
        - COORDINATE/COMMUNICATE PROGRAMS

- SUPPORT SPIRITUAL JOURNEY
- CONTINUE THE 6 MARKS OF DISCIPLESHIP
- DEVELOP GIFTS AND PASSIONS
- CELEBRATE EXISTING OUTREACH/MISSIONS
- EXPAND PARTICIPATION IN OUTREACH/MISSION PROGRAMS

4. **<u>ENHANCE WORSHIP EXPERIENCES</u>**
   - ▶ POSSIBILITIES:
     - PROVIDE FAMILY/CHILDREN FRIENDLY WORSHIP
     - GROW THE MUSIC PROGRAM
     - INCORPORATE MORE DRAMA
     - UNWRAP OUR GIFTS IN WORSHIP THROUGH:
       - INDIVIDUAL ARTS/POETRY/DRAMA
       - TESTIMONIALS
       - MUSIC
       - VISCOM
       - ETC.

5. **<u>ENHANCE YOUTH PROGRAM</u>**
   - ▶ GOAL: TO HAVE VIBRANT PROGRAMS FOR CHILDREN AND YOUTH WHERE THEY ARE ENGAGED AND VALUED THROUGHOUT IUCC
   - ▶ POSSIBILITIES:
     - ASKING QUESTIONS AND LISTENING TO THEIR RESPONSES
     - LEADERSHIP SUPPORTING THE CHILDREN/YOUTH
     - CONGREGATION ENGAGING CHILDREN/YOUTH
     - WORSHIP INVITING TO CHILDREN/YOUTH

6. **<u>IMPROVE COMMUNICATION</u>**
   - ▶ NEED A COMPREHENSIVE STRATEGY TO:
   - ▶ POSSIBILITIES:
     - REACH INTO THE COMMUNITY/PUBLIC RELATIONS
     - COORDINATE AND ENHANCE CURRENT METHODS OF COMMUNICATING

- PROVIDE INFORMATION THAT IS UP TO DATE
- PROVIDE INFORMATION THAT IS ACCURATE
- REACH ALL AGES AT IUCC

Under the leadership of Terra Osterling the Communication Team consisting of Kevin Branch, Nita Tischendorf, Ida Mangione, Dave and Maggie Ritchey, met in April and May of 2008.  The mission of the team was to facilitate Communication through the various IUCC media pieces and the outreach led to the Mid-Week announcement e-mail, the newsletter logistics, computer room/station for on-site web access to iuccspirit.com, outreach flyers and a redesign of the elements for the worship bulletin.

VISCOM (Visual Communications), under the direction of Steve Damtoft, Chip Izzo and Dan Reardon, continued to offer junior high and high school students a unique means of expression and a sense of belonging. VISCOM kicked off 2009 by shooting digital images at the Seneca Park Zoo, later to be edited and arranged to accompany a 1967 Simon & Garfunkel tune, "At the Zoo".

Photo taken on March 5, 2009

The century-old tradition of successful union of many denominations is one of the Sunday school's noteworthy characteristics. From the earliest moment of its inception in the minds of a Baptist, a Presbyterian and a Methodist, through all the long years of its community service, this idea has been successfully maintained and emphasized with the establishment of the church itself

***

In 2009, the Ruth Circle began in earnest to prepare for the IUCC Centennial and at the their meeting on September 15, 2009, the name for the year of events to celebrate 100 years was agreed on as the IUCC Centennial.  From identifying the events to take place, to discussing methods to incorporate in raising funds it was a group effort that promises a glorious way to look back in history and bring us forward to the future.

***

A hundred years is a long time, and the list of activities and achievements is long. It would take many volumes to record individually the names and works of all the men, women and children who have contributed to the life of the Sunday school and the church and many more to relate in detail the events that have provided a full program year after year.  All the programs and events that have become part of our history, continue on.  Active members who volunteer their services remain active in the church and its history.  Change has happened, but change has been for the better to keep our church active in meeting the needs of the community and the congregation during changing times.

Our hands reach out to all who are in need of our assistance. Our heart embraces your joy and your pain as you step forward into the future.

# ADDENDUM

On Saturday, May 30, 2015, our pastor, Rev. Michael Dack welcomed the community to our open house, highlighting the following changes made to the Irondequoit United Church of Christ.

New carpet in the sanctuary
New cushions in the sanctuary
Ceilings fans cleaned and painted
Painting of interior windows, doorways, walls and ceilings
New hardwood floor and redesign of the pulpit area
Pew aisles increased
New floor in entry way and hall way to sanctuary
New office structure off foyer to common room
New elevator and new entrance area at front east side of church
Major rehab of second floor/balcony
Upgrade electrical services
Upgrade fire alarm system
Enlarging doorway on 2nd floor to ADA compliant
Adding additional lighting on all three floors
Additional Flooring on all three floors
New doors on first and second floor
Asbestos removal
Remote entry controls and camera/intercom system
Additional insulation

| SUPERINTENDENTS  OF SUNDAY SCHOOL | |
| --- | --- |
| Samuel W. Lee | 1850 |
| Sidney B. Grant | 1851 |
| Mr. Brant | |
| D. R. Barton | 1852 |
| Mr. Adams | 1853 |
| Mr. Anderson | 1856 |
| W. R. Seward | 1857-1861* |
| Ezra Stanton | 1862-1867* |
| Alfred Benedict | 1868-1873* |
| Henry Achilles | 1874-1878 |
| George Rudman | 1878-1916 |
| Reuben A. Dake | 1917-1919 |
| Chauncey West | 1919-1922 |
| A. J. Warren | 1923-1927 |
| Loren Mason | 1928 |
| Samuel Russell | 1929-1930 |
| John Muxworthy | 1931 |
| John W. Thorne | 1932-1945 |
| Thorold G. Smith | 1946-1948 |
| Dr. Hewett W. Strever | 1949 |
| Robert E. Cortright | 1950 |
| **IUCC MINISTERS** | |
| Rev. Harold Capron | 1911-1916 |
| Rev. William J. Prout | 1917-1925 |
| Rev. Charles S. Bergner | 1925-1942 |
| Rev. Lloyd R. Stamp | 1943-1954 |
| Rev. Walter A. Telfer | 1955-1963 |
| Rev. Wilbour E. Saunders * | 1964 |
| Rev. Harleigh M. Rosenberger | 1965-1972 |
| Rev. Robert W. Bermudes | 1972-1993 |
| Rev. Ken Whitwer * | 1993-1995 |
| Rev. Jerry Alan Smith | 1995-2000 |
| Rev. Dale Davis | 2000-2008 |
| Rev. Janice Lee Fitzgerald * | 2008- |
| **ASSOCIATE MINISTERS** | |
| Rev. Joseph D. Billups | 1952-1954 |
| Rev. Howard S. Fuller | 1954-1957 |
| Rev. Leslie G Strathern | 1957--1962 |
| Rev. Donald M. Wilson | 1962-1969 |
| Rev. Charles K. Kuck | 1969-1973 |
| Rev. Richard D. Grobe | 1974-1983 |
| Rev. Thomas M. Schroeder | 1985-1987 |

| Rev. Andrew Overman  * | 1988 |
|---|---|
| Rev. Joan Turnbull | 1988-1990 |
| Rev. Cheryl Huff Slusser | 1990-1994 |
| Rev. Sherie Lindamood | 1994-1996 |
| Rev. Lynn Carman Bodden* | 1996-1998 |
| Rev, Sarah Culp | 1998-2000 |

*Approximate Dates

## * Interim

| Directors Of Christian Education | |
|---|---|
| Rev. Margaret Frerichs | 1956-1958 |
| Elizabeth Hyde Miller | 1959-1961 |
| Donna Maggi | 1961-1966 |
| Alice Bennides Kashuba | 1967-1969 |
| Henry Schwede | 1970-1975 |
| Rev. Richard Grobe | |
| Mary Record | 1975-1985 |
| Rev. Thomas Schroeder | |
| Marty Murray | |
| Pat Keltz | |
| Sharon L. Gass | 1985- |
| **Professional Music Directors/Organists** | |
| George Fisher Designer | |
| Mrs. Horace Blackwell | |
| Mr. M. Bliss Drake | |
| Mrs. Edwin Smallridge | William Crawford |
| Mrs. Chauncey West | Sylvia Aust |
| Lois Bell Benedict | Isabelle Francis |
| Rev. Charles Bergner | James Thrash |
| Ernest Robinson | Wilford Crawford |
| Lawrence Parker | Margaret Evans |
| Margaret Maxwell | Bruce & Kathy Beardsley |
| Dr. Ward Woodbury | Nina Woomert |
| Wilbur Sheridan | Jane S. Brinkman |
| Eugene Addams | Joe Gabalski |

# Directors Of Christian Education

| | |
|---|---|
| George & Barbara Klump | Colleen Curry |
| Joyce Caravetta | Bruce & Kathy Beardsley |
| | Nate Padget |

## Charter Members of United Congregational Church

Armstrong, Ezra
Armstrong, Alice M.
Andersen, Hjordes
Andersen, Kirsten
Anderson, Hugh McV.
Anderson, Mrs. Jacob
*Anderson, Grace
Anderson, Mable
Bell, Edgar
Bell, Mrs. Edgar
Bridgeman, Mrs. J.
Bogart, Guy H.
Bogart, Mrs. Guy H.
Cook, Harry
Cook, Mrs. Harry
Coy, Mrs. W. E.
Cole, Hattie
Cole, Ida M.
Clark, John
Clark, Samuel
Clark, William
Camping, Mrs. John
Camping, Gertrude
Camping, Matie
Cole, Mrs. Hylon
Dake, Reuben A.
Dake, Mrs. Maria
Disher, George
Disher, Mrs. George
Disher, Grace
Drake, M. Bliss
Drake, Mrs. M. B.
DeSmit, Daniel
DeSmit, Mrs. Daniel
Ernisse, Jay H.
Ernisse, Mrs. Jay H.
Franke, Abram
Franke, Mrs. A.
Fraser, James
Fraser, Mrs. Jas.
Fraser, Grace
Fraser, George
Fisher, Ray
Fisher, Mrs. Ray
Fisher, Mrs. Mary A.
Fritz, Clara
Fritz, Philip
Fritz, Mrs. Phil.
Fitt, George
Grant, Ina
Grant, Adeline
Grant, Frank
Grant, Mrs. Frank
Grant, Mrs. Theodore W.
Grant, Theo. W. Jr.
Graffrath, Rose
Graffrath, Ruth
Hammond, Frank
Heffer, Mr. Frank E.
Heffer, Mrs. Frank E.
Heffer, Spencer
Heffer, Mrs. Spencer
Heffer, Mrs. Louisa
Heffer, Harry
Heffer, Blanche
Heffer, Harvey
Heffer, Norris
Heffer, Everett

Heffer, John H.
Heffer, Mrs. John H.
Heffer, Wm. A.
Heffer, Mrs. Wm. A.
Heffer, Russell
Harding, George
Harding, Mrs. George
Harding, Harold
Harding, Raymond
Howard, James
Howard, Mrs. Jas.
Howard, Ray C.
Howard, Mrs. R. C.
Howard, Charles
Howard, Mrs. Chas.
Howard, Walter M.
Howard, Mrs. Walter M.
Howard, Nettie
Howard, William
Hallauer, George
Hallauer, Mrs. George
Hallauer, Everett
Hickson, Edwin
Hickson, Mrs. Edwin
Hill, William
Hill, Mrs. Wm.
Hill, Elva F.
Hill, Wilbur
Hill, Almond
Hill, W. Avery
Hewlett, Fred
Hewlett, Mrs. Fred
Hewlett, Mable
Hewlett, Laura
Hunt, George B.
Krompart, Ruby
List, Mrs. Adolph
List, Grace
List, George
List, Mrs. George
Leastman, Arthur
Leastman, Herbert
Leastman, Nellie
Leastman, Fred W.
Leake, Laura B.
Metcalfe, Fred B.
Metcalfe, Mrs. F. B.
Metcalfe, John
Metcalfe, Gladys
McKibbon, Mattie
Mortimer, Gladys
Marsh, Charles
Marsh, Mrs. Chas.
Muxworthy, Mrs. Alfred
Muxworthy, Mildred
Pengally, Thomas B.
Pengally, Mrs. T. B.
Peacock, John W.
Peacock, Mrs. John W.
Peacock, Harold
Peacock, John A.
Peacock, Frank
Peacock, Mrs. Frank
Peacock, Raymond
Peacock, Albert
Pammenter, James
Pammenter, Mrs. J.
Pammenter, May

Pammenter, Elmer
Pammenter, Arthur T.
Porter, Mrs. Chauncey
*Porter, Aura
Porter, Grace A.
Porter, Gladys J.
Porter, Ruth
Pendleton, Wm. A.
Pendleton, Mrs. Wm. A.
Platt, Charles
Platt, Mrs. Chas.
Platt, John
Platt, Frank H.
Platt, Raymond
Penlon, Arthur
Rayton, Joseph
Rayton, Mrs. Jos.
Rayton, Albert
Rayton, Mrs. Albert
Rayton, Vernie
Rayton, Herbert
Rayton, Mrs. Herbert
Rudman, Mrs. Wm. T.
Rudman, Roy S
Rudman, Mrs. Roy S.
Rudman, Wm. C.
Rudman, Mrs. Wm. C.
Rogers, Asenath
Rogers, Polly
Rogers, Ezra
Rogers, Mrs. Ezra
Smallridge, Fred J.
Smallridge, Mrs. F. J.
Sherman, Harry E.
Sherman, Mrs. H. E.
Strutt, Lillian
South, Walter
South, Mrs. Walter
South, Mrs. Chas. H.
South, Ray
Dodge, Archibold
Stanton, Harrison
Stanton, Estella
Stanton, Chester
Stanton, Mrs. Chester
Saunders, Arthur
Saunders, Mrs. Arthur
Saunders, Essie
Titus, Mrs. Emma
Titus, S. Leone
Titus, Seymour G.
Titus, Mrs. S. G.
Titus, Paul
West, George
West, Mrs. Geo.
West, Chauncey
West, Mrs. Chauncey
Warren, Almond J.
Warren, Mrs. A. J.
Warren, Stephen
Warren, Mrs. Stephen
Warren, Jas. H.
Warren, Anna
Warren, Bessie
Woods, Franklin B.
Woods, Mrs. Franklin B.
Walzer, Mrs. Harvey
*Marsh, Bessie